THE
ENGLISH
YOU NEED TO KNOW

Murray Bromberg
Director
SUPERCENTER, New York City Board of Education

Julius Liebb
Former Assistant Principal, English
Andrew Jackson High School, Queens, New York

BARRON'S EDUCATIONAL SERIES, INC.

New York · London · Toronto · Sydney

All inquiries should be addressed to:
Barron's Educational Series, Inc.
250 Wireless Boulevard
Hauppauge, New York 11788

Library of Congress Catalog Card No. 87-19446
International Standard Book No. 0-8120-2407-9

Library of Congress Cataloging-in-Publication Data

Bromberg, Murray.
    The English you need to know.

    Includes index.
    Summary: A writing and grammar textbook for the
development of reading and composition skills and the
introduction of basic grammar and usage.
    1. Readers—1950-   . 2. English language—Grammar
—1950-   . 3. English language—Composition and
exercises. [1. English language—Composition and
exercises. 2. English language—Grammar] I. Liebb,
Julius. II. Title.
PE1121.B694 1987   428.6   87-19446
ISBN 0-8120-2407-9

PRINTED IN THE UNITED STATES OF AMERICA

789 100 987654321

Table of Contents

Part I Reading and Writing

Part II Your Language Handbook

Introduction

THE ENGLISH YOU NEED TO KNOW is a unique, all-purpose book that was written to meet the multiple needs of today's students.

How is it unique? How all-purpose? What needs does it actually meet?

To start with, *THE ENGLISH YOU NEED TO KNOW* is divided into two parts — the first portion is devoted to reading, discussion, and composition skills, and the second is a language handbook which deals with the basics of English grammar and usage.

The unique quality of the book lies in its presentation of thirty interesting reading selections, many of them based on real-life situations. They are followed by thought-provoking discussion questions and carefully planned writing exercises that grow out of the articles and stories.

Furthermore, the language handbook material is related to the composition work. Grammar and punctuation exercises, clear and concise, are periodically keyed to earlier motivational sections, pointing up the interrelationship of the skills being taught.

This is an all-purpose text because the English teacher can use it throughout the year in a program of vocabulary building, reading comprehension, debating, composition, and technical English. A student who has successfully met the challenges presented in these pages will be ready for the rigors of the English courses that lie ahead.

Part I
Reading and Writing

- Stories for Discussion
- Reading Comprehension
- Writing Insights
- Vocabulary

Lesson 1
NARRATION I

NOW YOU SEE IT...

On my first day at Filmore High School I found more excitement than I had bargained for. Shortly after being seated in my homeroom, I reached into the desk to store my new notebook and my fingers touched an object that was cold and metallic. Moving it toward me, but carefully protecting it from the gaze of my fellow students, I saw that it was a handgun.

Naturally, I was frightened. The closest I had ever come to a gun before was playing with my water pistol when I was six years old. But this was the real thing. When I looked around, it seemed that everyone else was busy filling out book receipts. I decided that as soon as the class had left the room I would turn the gun over to my teacher.

All sorts of wild thoughts were running through my mind. Had the gun been used in a crime? Were there fingerprints on it? Would the police believe my story? Was I going to get blamed for something?

I wasn't listening to the teacher's instructions, but she must have been talking about fire drill regulations because in a moment the gongs began to go off, and everyone rose dutifully to march out of the building.

I pushed the gun in as far as it could go, covered it with my notebook, and joined the end of the line just as the teacher was about to scold me for dragging my feet. In a fog, I staggered down the stairs, across the lawn, and out onto the street. My active imagination was recalling all the TV mystery shows I had seen. Could I have stumbled on a murder weapon? Whose gun was it? What was going on? Could I get into trouble?

After the fire drill was over, we re-entered the building. Now I raced up the stairs, stepping on the heels of the slowpoke ahead of me. Even the teacher remarked about my haste to return to the classroom.

As soon as I was seated, I thrust my hand into the desk. It wasn't there! It wasn't there! I looked around quickly, feeling everyone's eyes on my neck. Once again my hand explored the inside of the desk. I bent over and looked. It was definite — the gun was gone.

I was out of my seat in a flash, heading for the teacher's desk, when a redheaded girl across the aisle tripped me up. She leaned over me as I lay sprawled on the floor and hissed in my ear, "You didn't see a thing. Get it, Shorty?"

I nodded, picked myself up slowly, and went back to my seat. So far I haven't told a soul about the disappearing gun. I don't want to get involved.

Did you enjoy the story? Most people who read this story find it enjoyable, and they are eager to find out more about what happened.

Everyone loves a good story.

And everyone loves to listen to a good storyteller.

On the other hand, no one listens to a bad storyteller for very long.

You can learn to be a good storyteller and have people enjoy listening to you and reading what you write. All you have to do is learn to follow the few simple rules you will find here and in the following lessons.

TO BEGIN

Below is a scrambled list of the important events that happened in the story "Now You See It..." Put the events in the order in which they took place, looking back at the story if you find it necessary.

2 1.   I found a handgun in my desk.
7 2.   The girl across the aisle tripped me up and said "You didn't see a thing."
4 3.   The class left the room for a fire drill.
5 4.   I hurried back when the class re-entered the building.
1 5.   I entered homeroom for my first day in high school.
3 6.   I decided to turn the gun in to the teacher when the class left the room.
8 7.   I haven't told anyone about the disappearing gun because I don't want to get involved.
6 8.   The gun was gone from the desk. .

TO REMEMBER

Now that you have put the events in correct order, notice how the very interesting story is built up around eight important events.

That is the clue to the first rule for good storytelling!

Tell what happened clearly, and in logical order. Usually, that means telling it in *chronological* order, the order in which the events actually happened.

Before you write a story (another name for storytelling is *narration*), it helps to have a clear idea of the events of the story and the order in which they happened.

YOUR TURN

A.   Here is an outline of a story written by a student. Read it over and then try to write the story from the outline. Imagine the details.

1.   I came back from school and found the house empty.
2.   "Anybody home?" I called.
3.   A strong, dangerous-looking man appeared at the top of the stairs with our TV set in his hands.
4.   I turned and ran for the door.
5.   When I turned the doorknob, it came off in my hands.
6.   I tried to force the door open but only succeeded in falling flat on my face.
7.   The man came up to me and screamed.
8.   He said, "I'm the TV repair man. Your folks know I'm here."
9.   He helped me up.
10.   My parents came home.
11.   We got the doorknob repaired.

B.   Think of something that happened to you that could make an interesting story. It could be a recent event, or something way back in the past.

Some tips:

1. It's best if the event took a very short time — ten minutes, or an hour. Don't go beyond a day or a week.
2. Think of something unusual, surprising, embarrassing, or painful; an experience that turned from bad to good, or good to bad; something that you learned a lesson from, or that taught someone else a lesson; a time when you or someone you knew was in danger. It could be something you would have wanted to tell someone about right after it happened, or perhaps something you have kept secret all these years but now are willing to tell about.

Now, write down the important things that happened, in the order in which they took place — just as was done in *Your Turn*, above.

Write the story in as interesting a way as you can. Look back at the story "Now You See It..." for clues as to how to tell an interesting story.

C. Finish the story, "Now You See It..." adding your idea of how it might have developed.

NOUNS

In order to write well, you must learn the tools of the trade. All language is divided into parts of speech which you must learn to use to the best advantage. Let's begin with nouns.

The following list contains nouns from Lesson One. You should be able to find many more.

day
Filmore High School
object
gaze
thought
crime
instructions
trouble
flash

Study the section on nouns in the Language Handbook (p. 111) and complete the exercises to begin your mastery of English.

EXPANDING YOUR VOCABULARY

Ten useful vocabulary words from the story are in Column A below. Find their meanings in Column B. It might help you to turn back to the story to reread the sentences in which these words appeared.

A	B
F 1. definite	a. sight
I 2. dutifully	b. brought into difficulty; entangled
C 3. explored	c. searched
A 4. gaze (n)	d. pushed
H 5. haste	e. find fault with
B 6. involved	f. clear, certain
D 7. thrust	g. moved unsteadily
J 8. regulations	h. speed
E 9. scold	i. obediently
G 10. staggered	j. rules

5

Lesson 2
NARRATION II

THE GUN IN THE DESK

Three weeks had passed since my first day at Filmore High School. I kept my mouth shut about the gun which had appeared momentarily in my desk and then mysteriously vanished during the fire drill. The red-haired girl who had frightened me into silence glared in my direction for the first few days but she had been absent regularly since then. Slowly I began to erase the troublesome incident from my consciousness, and my fear began to fade.

"GUN SOUGHT IN ARMORED CAR ROBBERY. GUARD SHOT"

The startling headline in our local paper during the last week in September brought the whole story back to my mind with a rush. Three masked young thieves, one of them thought to be a red-haired girl, had held up an armored car and wounded its driver in the course of the robbery. He was in critical condition, given only a 50-50 chance to survive. If the gun could be recovered, the police said, they would have an excellent chance of identifying the thieves and capturing them.

What to do? Should I inform on the girl? Maybe it was just a coincidence? My parents had always cautioned me to stay out of trouble. What to do?

The next day, I was surprised to see the redheaded girl in school. Summoning up all my nerve I said to her, "I'm going to tell about the gun."

"How old are you?" she asked.

"Fifteen."

"If you want to be sixteen, you'll forget about it. We know where you live."

The tone of her voice was so threatening that my courage flew out the window. I came home that afternoon more mixed up than ever but determined not to stick my neck out.

My parents went to play bingo that evening, leaving me alone to do my homework. It was no use. How could I concentrate on geometry when the vision of that gun kept blotting out my textbook? Suddenly there came a knocking at the door.

"Who's there?" I stammered.

"Open up, we want to talk to you." It was a girl's voice.

I ran to the back of the house to slip out through the kitchen. Just as I opened the door a man tried to force his way in. I slammed the door on his leg and darted back to the living room, turning out all the lights as I ran.

I picked up the phone and was dialing the police when I heard the window glass being broken in the front parlor. I crawled behind the door and as the girl and her partner came through the window I fled out the front door in my stockinged feet, going 40 miles an hour, my heart pounding like a jackhammer in my chest.

At the corner of Main and Maple Streets I ran headlong into traffic and was almost run over by a cruising police car. The chase was over; the thieves would be caught. In talking to the detectives later, I heard how my unwillingness to get involved had led to the near death of the armored car driver. It was an expensive way for me to get an education, but I learned the terrible price of fear.

FROM ME TO YOU (Writing a Narration)

Here is another way the story might have been written. Read it over and decide whether it is as interesting as the original. Then try to draw up some reasons for preferring one story or the other.

Three weeks had passed and I began to forget the mysterious gun in the desk. After the first few days, the redheaded girl was absent from class.

Then I read in the newspaper about an armored car robbery where the driver had been shot and had only a 50-50 chance of living. One of the robbers was thought to be a redheaded girl!

I didn't know what to do. Then, the next day, the girl was back in school. I told her I was going to tell about the gun. She threatened me. That made me change my mind about saying anything.

I was alone that night when a man and a girl tried to break into our house. I managed to get away and reach a cruising patrol car. The thieves were caught. The armored car driver lived, but I had learned a lesson about the price of fear.

Which story did you like better?
Most readers prefer the first story. Why?
Perhaps the first story sounds more real, and is more exciting. You want to keep reading to find out what will happen next.
The author of the first story has done three important things to make the story interesting.
1. You want to find out what will happen next: this is called *suspense*. 2. The story seemed real because of *specific details*. 3. You were made to think that you were right at the scene, overhearing it all, through the use of *direct quotation*.

Suspense

The author keeps you interested because you want to know the answers to questions:
1. Was the gun used in the robbery the one the narrator (the teller of the story) had seen in the desk?
2. Was the girl in the class involved in the robbery?
3. Should the narrator have told about the gun?
4. Will the people who try to break into the house succeed in harming the narrator?
5. Will the narrator manage to get away from them?

To Do

1. Copy three sentences from the story that help to keep you in suspense.
2. Go back over the story you wrote at the end of the last lesson. Does it have enough suspense? Think of some ways you might add more suspense to it.

Specific Details

The good storyteller tells the story in such a way that the reader feels present at the scene. Specific details help to give the reader this feeling of *reality* (being real). If you write "an old car," you leave the picture vague. It seems more real if you are more specific and write "a dusty yellow Pinto, with rust eating away at the edges."

To Do

1. Copy three sentences from the story that seem particularly real to you.
2. Look at the first sentence of the last paragraph: "At the corner of Main and Maple Streets I ran headlong into traffic and was almost run over by a cruising police car." Would the story be improved by more specific detail at this point? Make up two sentences that would be more specific than the sentence from the story.
3. Go back over the story you wrote at the end of the last lesson. Is there enough specific detail? Try to add more in at least three places.

Direct Quotation

Using the exact words of a speaker also helps to make a story seem real. Would the story have been less interesting if instead of this use of direct quotation (called *dialogue* when two or more people speak with one another), the second passage had been used instead?

1. Summoning up all my nerve, I said to her, "I'm going to tell about the gun."
   "How old are you?" she asked.
      "Fifteen."
      "If you want to be sixteen, you'll forget about it. Besides, we know where you live."

2. I told her I was going to tell about the gun. She threatened me.

Why is the direct quotation better than the second passage?

To Do

1. In the last paragraph of the story, one sentence reads, "In talking to the detectives later, I learned how my unwillingness to get involved had led to the near death of the armored car driver." Would the story have been better if this had been written out as direct quotation, as a dialogue between the narrator and the detectives? Why?
2. Write the dialogue that might have taken place between the narrator and the detectives.
3. Go back over the story you wrote at the end of the last lesson. Are there places where direct quotation would help the story? See if you can find at least one place where you can add a direct quotation; then, write out that added direct quotation.

YOUR TURN

Rewrite the entire story you wrote at the end of the last lesson, making use of the additions you have made for suspense, specific detail and direct quotation.

PRONOUNS

Following are some pronouns (words that can substitute for nouns) taken from Lesson Two. Can you locate others?

my
I
which
who
them
its

The second part of the Language Handbook deals with pronouns (page 116). Personal pronouns are easy to spot. Relative pronouns may prove more challenging. The Handbook will show you how to choose the correct form of a pronoun every time.

EXPANDING YOUR VOCABULARY

Choose the correct meaning for each of these ten words from the story.

1. *cautioned* me   a) beckoned b) warned c) hastened
2. just a *coincidence*   a) chance happening b) lucky circumstance c) omen
3. erase...from my *consciousness*   a) awareness b) common sense c) intelligence
4. in *critical* condition   a) finding fault b) reasonable c) dangerous
5. *glared* in my direction   a) looked angrily b) erupted c) glanced
6. troublesome *incident*   a) complication b) event c) conclusion
7. appeared *momentarily*   a) for a short while b) precisely c) importantly
8. *summoning* up all my nerve   a) considering b) calling c) relying upon
9. a 50-50 chance to *survive*   a) remain alive b) regain health c) succeed
10. mysteriously *vanished*   a) polished b) appeared c) disappeared

Lesson 3
DESCRIPTION

HAVING FUN IN OUR TOWN

It's 5 p.m. on a sultry July day in our town. The heat is still steaming up from the pavement. The doors of the casino open wide and out comes a steady stream of people, shuffling and blinking, into the sunlight. Each man and woman is clutching a dice-spotted box of pastel salt-water taffy, compliments of the management, a little going-away gift to help them forget about the dreams that didn't quite come true. Obediently crossing at the corner, the caravans of ants head toward the buses for the long journey back to civilization.

As early as 7 o'clock that morning they had lined up to board the huge buses (air-conditioned with rest rooms in the rear) which would carry them to our town, the place where the action is. Nervously they had joked about hitting the slot machine jackpots or breaking the bank at the roulette tables. Although the bus driver had heard it all before, he still managed a polite smile. Every morning he sees the play acted out — a different cast of characters but the same dialogue.

"My sister and I have a system. We wait for the slot machine someone has just quit because it didn't pay off, and we stick at it until we hit the big one (100 quarters)."

"I don't expect to gamble. I'll just walk around and soak up the atmosphere."

"I'm going to drop my $40 and consider it my investment for a full day of entertainment."

"Blackjack is my game. I can remember the cards that just came out, and that gives me the edge over the house's dealer."

We see them pulling into the spacious parking lots around 11 each morning. They are only slightly rumpled from the long bus ride and able to move swiftly into the casinos. In their hands are the green vouchers which entitle them to a free buffet. There are twenty-five different kinds of colorful pies and gooey cakes at the end of the lunch line, all tasting exactly the same. Nobody seems to mind, or even notice. Within a few minutes, they are all hypnotized in the darkness, pulling the levers without emotion, sprinkling their betting chips on the dice tables, moving restlessly around the football fields in search of the machine which is ready to pay off big, the lucky table, the pot of gold.

"You should have been here last week," the bus driver confides. "One of our regular passengers won $6500."

It's 5:30 p.m. on a sultry July day in our town. I wave goodby to an old couple, crowned with scarlet Texaco golf hats, slumped in the back of their bus. They stare back at me, blankly. They have had a long and tiring day.

TIME TO REMEMBER AND REFLECT

1. What going-away gift did all the casinos give to their customers?

2. How high was the slot machines' big jackpot?

3. What was the explanation offered by the traveler who planned to lose his $40?

4. Why weren't the gamblers upset about the buffet lunch?

5. Why didn't the bus driver say that very few of his passengers ever came home a winner?

6. Is the title of the story, "Having Fun In Our Town," an accurate one? Why was it used? Can you suggest a better title?

7. "They ought to close down those gambling places," a waitress said. "I hate to see the senior citizens losing their hard-earned savings there." Tell why you agree or disagree with her statement.

CREATING VIVID PICTURES

Descriptive writing is used to paint word pictures of people, places, objects, and scenes. When it is done well, such writing stays with us for a long time and can be more satisfying than much narration or exposition.

Being Selective

The descriptive writer is like the skillful user of a camera. Alfred Eisenstadt, one of the most celebrated photographers of our time, has pointed out that his success can be attributed to his ability to focus on what is significant in a face or a landscape. Painters, poets, photographers, and writers must know what to highlight and what to exclude. You can't put in everything. You have to decide what is important for the scene you are describing, and what can be ignored.

Selection...Specificity

After you have chosen the main parts of the scene being described, you must move on to the specific details which will help bring it to life. In "Having Fun in Our Town," we learn the following:

It's 5 p.m., a hot and moist July day, heat steaming up from the pavement. People leaving the casinos don't merely carry a "gift" but they are clutching "a dice-spotted box of pastel salt-water taffy." They do more than "exit from the casinos" — they come out "shuffling and blinking into the sunlight." We don't see mere lines of people returning to their buses but "caravans of ants." The defeated old couple in the last paragraph are "crowned with scarlet Texaco golf hats," adding to the unreal quality of the scene. All of those specific details help us to visualize the scene in this gambling city and to form an opinion about it.

MASTERS OF DESCRIPTION

Charles Dickens and Feodor Dostoyevski were masters of the art of description. Readers of their novels are presented with visual treats, page after page. The following two selections are fine examples of the descriptive technique. As you read them, be prepared to explain their strengths:

Mr. Squeer's appearance was not prepossessing. He had but one eye, and the popular prejudice runs in favour of two. The eye he had was unquestionably useful, but decidedly not ornamental: being of a greenish gray, and in shape resembling the fan-light of a street door. The blank side of his face was much wrinkled and puckered up, which gave him a very sinister appearance, especially when he smiled, at which times his expression bordered closely on the villainous. His hair was very flat and shiny, save at the ends, where it was brushed stiffly up from a low protruding forehead, which assorted well with his harsh voice and coarse manner. He was about two or three and fifty, and a trifle below the middle size; he wore a white neck-erchief with long ends, and a suit of scholastic black; but his coat sleeves, being a great deal too short, he appeared ill at ease in his clothes, and as if he were in a perpetual state of aston-ishment at finding himself so respectable.

from *Nicholas Nickleby* by Charles Dickens

Did You Note

the frightening aspects of the one-eyed man?
the careful description of his hair?
the treatment of Squeer's clothing?
his wrinkles?
the way the author begins with a single detail, and builds to a picture of the whole man?

Is there enough in this thumbnail description for an artist to paint Mr. Squeer's description? Why? Does the description give you an idea of Mr. Squeer's personality as well as of his appearance? If you had to get an actor prepared to play Mr. Squeer's role, would you have enough help from Dickens to proceed with the production? Is this an objective description or an interpretation?

The old woman was, as usual, bare-headed. Her thin fair hair, just turning grey, and thick with grease, was plaited into a rat's tail and fastened into a knot above her nape with a frag-ment of horn comb. Because she was so short the axe struck her full on the crown of her head. She cried out, but very feebly, and sank in a heap to the floor, still with enough strength left to raise both hands to her head. One of them still held the "pledge." Then he struck her again and yet again, with all his strength, always with the blunt side of the axe, and always on the crown of the head. Blood poured out as if from an overturned glass and the body toppled on its back. He stepped away as it fell, and then stooped to see the face: she was dead. Her wide-open eyes looked ready to start out of their sockets, her forehead was wrinkled and her whole face convulsively distorted.

from *Crime and Punishment* by Feodor Dostoyevski

Did You Note

the careful description of the woman's hair?
the body's position?
the actions of both characters?
the way the attention shifts back and forth between the old woman and her attacker?

In what ways would a movie director be guided to a successful filming of the murder, based on Dostoevsky's graphic description? Is this an objective description or an interpretation?

YOUR TURN

A. Decide on a subject for description: a place, an object, a person. Make up your mind as to the image you wish to convey. Is it the *stillness* of a museum, the *sense of humor* of an uncle, the *complexity* of a gadget? List some specific details which should be included — but remember to be selective. Then write a descriptive piece of about 200 words.

B. Complete *one* of the following. Choose descriptive details which will help us to see the place as you see it.

1. "Our school cafeteria is a zoo."
2. "My cousin is a train collector whose cellar looks like the busiest depot in the world."
3. "We wandered into the silent graveyard at midnight."

C. Consult copies of the two books by Dickens and Dostoyevski. Locate two more descriptive passages in each book and copy them in your own hand. Pay close attention to the writer both as a camera eye and as an interpreter of what can be seen through the camera's lens.

VERBS

steams
is clutching
head
had lined up
soak up
entitle
tastes
will be
are hypnotized

After studying the verb section in the Handbook (page 000) find other verbs in this lesson. Be careful not to select verbals (infinitives, participles, gerunds) which will be discussed in a later chapter. There are many details to learn about verbs but it is worth the effort. Remember that verbs carry your thoughts. They pack the power in your sentences.

EXPANDING YOUR VOCABULARY

Match the vocabulary words from the story in Column A with the meanings in Column B.

A	B
1. atmosphere	a. advantage
2. blankly	b. lines of travelers on a journey
3. buffet (n)	c. neighborhood conditions
4. caravans	d. seated in a drooping manner
5. edge	e. without seeing
6. rumpled	f. hot and moist
7. slumped	g. serve-yourself meal
8. spacious	h. wrinkled; disordered
9. sultry	i. receipt
10. voucher	j. roomy

Lesson 4
EXPOSITION I

WHY SO LATE?

Are you often late for school or work?

Psychologists say that lateness is rarely an accident. More likely it is connected to unconscious feelings about school or your job. You may be bored, and lateness is your way of expressing your resistance to wasting your time. Or, if you feel insecure because of poor achievement, lateness is your way of saying "no" to an unhappy situation. Then again, you may resent authority. You want to feel free, unhampered by rules, regulations, bells, time clocks, and ID cards. Any one of these could account for your tardiness.

There are as many alibis as there are explanations for chronic lateness to school or to work. Professor Susan Shnidman of Harvard Medical School has studied the problem for several years and in the course of her work has heard some imaginative excuses for lateness:

"I took the garbage out. The door locked behind me. It took an hour to find the superintendent to open the door."

"My astrologer advised me not to get out of bed before noon today."

"We wall-papered our living room last night and I couldn't find the front door."

"My brother has the measles. I had to deliver his newspapers this morning."

Perhaps the most fanciful excuse Prof. Shnidman ever uncovered was, "A snow flake flew into my watch and slowed down the mechanism."

In order to overcome frequent tardiness, psychologists advise the following:
a) Be aware that it is an undesirable habit that may hurt you and those you love.
b) Decide to change your ways.
c) Keep a daily log of your activities. Analyze it to see where you could save time.
d) Divide your tasks into "must do" and "not necessary to do at this time."
e) Set your watch ahead. Trick yourself into being on time.

TIME TO REMEMBER AND REFLECT

1. What do psychologists say about people who are frequently late for work?

2. Which alibi for lateness had something to do with a brother's illness?

3. Which alibi for lateness was "the most fanciful excuse" Professor Shnidman ever uncovered?

4. Why is a well-organized person less likely to be late?

5. According to psychologists, how do people who are often late react to authority?

6. List two useful suggestions to help someone overcome frequent lateness.

7. When was the last time you were late for an appointment? What was the reason for it? Did you lie about your lateness? Why?

EXPOSITORY WRITING

Some of the stories we read are suspenseful, in the manner of "Now You See It…" Some use autobiography, in the manner of "The Baked Potato" which you will come to shortly in Lesson 6; they tell a true story in order to make a point. Both appeal to our emotions and are successful to the degree that we care about what happens to the people in the story.

Most of our writing, however, is of the essay or composition variety. We take a topic, research and analyze it, and then serve it up to the reader in straightforward form. Often, information is presented which lies beyond the experience or knowledge of most readers. This is called *expository writing*: it sets forth facts, ideas and explanations.

Expository writing is different from the narration, found in the first two lessons in this book, which tells a story. Here is a description of three selections which appear in future lessons. Tell why you think the selection is *narrative* or *expository*:

1. Two brothers are barred from Little League competition.
2. The competition among Chinese students for admission to college is very fierce.
3. A Hungarian inventor claims to have found a cure for baldness.

Requirements of Exposition

Expository writing is often harder to do than narration. In narration, the story unfolds in logical order as you move from event to event. It is relatively easy to organize. But in exposition, you have to decide on your own organization. You must be prepared to lay out clearly the process or the idea which you want to explain to your audience.

The organization of "Why So Late?" is simple and effective. It consists of three parts:

1. Psychologists' explanations of people's tardiness
2. Some far-fetched alibis
3. Suggestions to help chronic latecomers

To Do

Any one of these segments could serve as the topic of a piece of expository writing. Choose either 1, 2, or 3, and develop it into a three-paragraph expository essay.

YOUR TURN

Write an expository article on *one* of the following:

1. The Best Way to Do Homework
2. Managing a Teenager's Budget
3. The Appeal of Country and Western Music

Before You Start Writing…

When you write an expository article, you need a good introductory paragraph. Naturally, there are hundreds of ways to do an introductory paragraph (Lesson 6 has more to say about this subject) **15** but some ingredients are constant. You should arouse the reader's interest as well as make a general statement about the issue you are dealing with. Challenging statements, provocative questions, humorous comments, eye-raising statistics, paradoxical remarks — all are possible openers. What is most important, however, is that the readers should not have to read too many lines before they know where you are taking them.

Tell what weaknesses and strengths you find in these opening lines for the above topics:

1. "I'd rather have a tooth extracted than do homework, but I have found a way to survive in school nevertheless."
2. "Like every other fellow and girl in my crowd, I'm continually broke."
3. "Keep your Beethoven, Bach, Gershwin, and Berlin. Just give me a gee-tar, a ten-gallon hat, and a cowboy's lament, and I'm in heaven."

ADJECTIVES

unconscious
insecure
unhampered
chronic
several
imaginative
this

These words taken from Lesson Four give you some idea how adjectives can sharpen your writing. Locate other adjectives in the story. The facts on adjectives are laid out fully in the Handbook (page 128). Complete the exercises and watch your writing begin to sparkle.

EXPANDING YOUR VOCABULARY

Choose the correct meaning for each of these words from "Why So Late."

1. you may resent *authority*   a) organization   b) those who have power   c) royalty
2. *chronic* lateness   a) sick   b) never stopping   c) unexcused
3. you feel *insecure*   a) lacking in confidence   b) uneasy   c) complacent
4. slowed down the *mechanism*   a) network   b) repairs   c) working parts of a machine
5. *psychologists* say   a) those who study behavior   b) experts   c) professors
6. lateness *rarely* is an accident   a) usually   b) sometimes   c) hardly ever
7. *resent* authority   a) feeling angry at   b) happened yesterday   c) praise
8. account for your *tardiness*   a) good health   b) sincerity   c) lateness
9. *unconscious* feelings   a) sleeping   b) not knowing   c) hurt
10. *unhampered* by rules   a) not bound   b) closed in   c) restricted

Lesson 5
EXPOSITION II

DOCTOR SHANNA

Almost all of the colleges in this country can be regarded as respectable institutions. In return for tuition money, they offer a variety of useful courses and, ultimately, a degree for those who qualify. There are a few colleges, however, that operate in a shady manner, providing degrees to which people are not entitled, for courses that they never took. One of the most notorious in recent years was Pacific College in Los Angeles, California, sometimes called "the dropouts' Harvard."

To illustrate how easy it was to get an advanced degree from such "diploma mills," New York legislator Leonard Stavisky enrolled his German shepherd, Shanna, at Pacific College. "Ms. Shanna Stavisky" presumably sent in her admission fee of $150 and by return mail received a breezy letter from "Dean Ashby" that read, "Your talent and experience are going to be recognized sooner or later. Welcome, my friend, to Pacific College."

Shanna was placed in a Ph.D. program in "recreation management." "That is very appropriate," joked Mr. Stavisky, "since Shanna has had field experience in the backyard and supervises child recreation because she is a watchdog."

The reason for interest in the case is that some citizens who need degrees to gain employment can bluff their way through by producing phony degrees that they bought from disreputable institutions. "How would you like to undergo brain surgery at the hands of someone who had gotten his medical certification from Pacific College?" asked one of Stavisky's assistants.

Mr. Stavisky's committee kept a close eye on all degree-offering institutions in New York. Some states, however, have been lax in supervising the diploma mills. Mr. Stavisky is hoping for a national crackdown on all crooks in the education field.

"I knew Shanna couldn't be a Ph.D.," said Mr. Stavisky. "After all, she flunked out of obedience school."

TIME TO REMEMBER AND REFLECT

1. Why was Pacific College referred to as "the dropouts' Harvard"?

2. Into what kind of Ph.D. program did the college place "Ms. Shanna Stavisky"?

3. Why did Mr. Stavisky think that the college had made a wise choice about Shanna's area of specialization?

4. Why is a New York legislator interested in a California diploma mill?

5. What humorous explanation did Mr. Stavisky offer to show his disbelief in Shanna's success at Pacific College?

6. Mr. X bought an advanced degree from Pacific College and is now a respected vice-president of a medical supply company. If his boss finds out the truth, should he fire Mr. X? Why?

7. "Every few years we crack down on these diploma factories," admitted a California legislator, "but they come out of the woodwork as soon as our backs are turned." Should anything be done about organizations such as Pacific College? What specific recommendations could you make?

EXPOSITORY WRITING

A critical first step in the process of exposition is to decide on the limits of your subject. "Careers," for example, is too broad a topic, unless you intend to write an encyclopedia. Begin cutting down the size of the topic until you have reached one that can be covered in the time and space limits given. Some limited possibilities for careers are "Beautician" or "Auto Mechanic." The general topic of "Diplomas" could be limited to "Recent Change in Diploma Requirements."

Purpose

After properly narrowing your subject, your second step is the formulation of a point of view. State briefly and clearly what you plan to say about your topic, whether you are explaining how to operate a specific computer, telling who won an election for governor in New Jersey, or analyzing the need to reexamine U.S. policy towards Cuba. The topic sentence, a succinct summary of the point you want to develop, is a necessary ingredient of clear, responsible writing. Without it, a paragraph may seem haphazard, hit-or-miss, and unsure of where it is heading.

Finally, a writer of a good expository composition takes pains to develop the topic with concrete examples, interesting illustrations, cogent reasons, or revealing details. Too many student compositions do not develop, expand, or illustrate a basic idea but merely repeat the topic sentence, sometimes in three or four different ways. The best way to avoid this error is to make certain that each sentence adds to, clarifies, or broadens the original thought instead of merely restating it.

To Do

What, in your opinion, are the strengths and weaknesses of the following student paragraph? Use the following questions to help you evaluate the paragraph.

1. Has the author of this paragraph chosen a topic that can be handled in a single paragraph?

2. Is the author's point of view clear?

3. Does the author develop the topic with concrete examples or illustrations?

4. Does the author do more than simply repeat the topic sentence?

Television has become the problem as well as the solution in education. Children spend too much time watching TV, but some programs are helpful. They may have learned a lot from TV but they can't resist turning on the TV as soon as they get home. Certainly no educator would object to the dramatizations of famous books or the televising of important news events. Still, is there any educational value in sitting in front of the "boob tube" for three hours watching a football game? Television is a coin with two sides and it's a toss-up whether it does more harm or good.

Development

The article entitled "Dr. Shanna" is worth studying as a model of exposition. Its first sentence begins to draw the limits of the topic by conceding that while most colleges are respectable and offer degrees to those who qualify, a few colleges operate in a shady manner. This idea provides the topic sentence and point of view for the entire selection. To prove the point, the article relates Mr. Stavisky's success in registering his dog Shanna for a Ph.D. program in Pacific College. There is no pointless repetition of the theme stated earlier. Instead you see an extreme instance of a "diploma mill" in action.

Though there is a humorous aspect to this "shaggy dog" story, the author underscores the seriousness of the problem by suggesting that with the help of these disreputable institutions, people have obtained jobs for which they are unqualified. The references to Pacific College "surgeons" indicates the public may be endangered by such phony schools, and the call for a national policy on "educational crooks" leaves no doubt about the author's views on the subject.

All this does much more than simply repeat the topic sentence. "Doctor Shanna" demonstrates how to limit a topic, present a point of view, and develop a topic sentence with an illustrative incident that has both a humorous twist and a serious approach to ending such fraud in the field of education.

THE THREE-PART CONSTRUCTION

Following some of the reading selections in this book are writing exercises that call for essays of at least three paragraphs. The best advice for young writers is to regard the opening paragraph as an *introduction* to the topic. You might imagine yourself in a helicopter on your way into the landing zone. You are, in essence, approaching the theme in the initial series of related sentences that make up the first paragraph.

To carry out the metaphor, in the middle paragraph you are on the ground, coming to grips with the topic in what is usually referred to as the *development* of the essay.

Finally, in the last paragraph you are flying above the topic — seeing it in broad perspective as you depart the scene and make some closing remarks on the theme of the composition. This is called the *conclusion*.

This three-part construction could be expanded to four, five, six or more paragraphs. Usually, it is the development that is expanded; the first and last paragraphs will remain as introduction and conclusion. Of course, the helicopter concept is a simplified way of looking at the problem, but students often find it to be a useful analogy.

YOUR TURN

A. For each general topic suggest a limited topic.

Example: (General) Space Exploration (Limited) The Most Recent Space Voyage of Columbia
1. School problems
2. Foreign policy
3. Music
4. Police
5. Books

B. Discuss the appropriateness of the following titles for a 250-word composition:

1. An Exciting World Series
2. The Volunteer Army
3. My Favorite Pastime
4. Our President
5. Peace in the Middle East

C. Write a topic sentence for each of the following titles that suggests a point of view:

    1. How to be energy efficient
    2. Food fads
    3. Spring
    4. Our football team's chances for a championship
    5. My pet peeve

D. Now, beginning with any title suggested in this chapter, write a 250-word composition in three paragraphs, developing your point of view with examples, details, explanations, illustrations, and/or stories.

EXPANDING YOUR VOCABULARY

Match the vocabulary word for the story in Column A with the meaning in Column B.

A	B
1. bluff (v)	a. well known, but usually for bad reasons
2. disreputable	b. careless; not strict
3. illustrate	c. finally
4. lax	d. to deceive
5. notorious	e. play or amusement
6. presumably	f. payment for instruction
7. recreation	g. having a bad reputation
8. respectable	h. honest; decent
9. tuition	i. make clear
10. ultimately	j. probably

Lesson 6
INTRODUCTIONS

THE BAKED POTATO

A baked potato and a father's love. That's an unlikely combination — and yet to Jack Sheradsky it is very meaningful.

Turn back the calendar to November of 1942, the time of World War II. Jack was 14 years old. He and his father were inmates assigned to hard labor at a Nazi concentration camp in Majdank, Poland. The Germans were systematically working them to death and starving them to death at the same time. Their daily food ration was muddy coffee, watery soup made of weeds, and a thin slice of moldy bread.

Although his father was lucky enough to have been chosen to toil indoors, Jack had to struggle in freezing temperatures digging ditches, unloading freight cars, and building roads. Unless he got more nourishing food, it was only a matter of time before he would be too frail to work. Once that happened, he could expect to be sent to the gas chamber.

One cold day, Jack's father managed to slip a warm, round object to the boy. It was a baked potato, smuggled out of the guards' kitchen. Jack's father was desperately hungry himself, but he saved the potato for his son. There was another potato for Jack the next day. And the next.

A baked potato. An insignificant baked potato to which we pay little attention today became the most important item in Jack Sheradsky's life. He dreamed about it, nibbled on it for hours under his blanket after lights out at night, and looked forward to his father's gift all through the brutal work day.

And then the Germans tightened their kitchen control so that it was impossible for Jack's father to steal the treasured potatoes. The boy's entire world crumbled before him — his one "luxury" had been withdrawn.

It wasn't until the war was over and Jack was much older that he realized the full significance of his father's gift. The life-sustaining potato had been reserved for Jack in the classical gesture of sacrifice that a parent makes for a child.

In later years, the image of the potato would be vivid in Jack's mind as he deprived himself, in a sense, in order to help put his own children through college. He knew that with such a tradition, his own children would pass on their baked potatoes when the time came.

TIME TO REMEMBER AND REFLECT

1. What was the daily ration served to the inmates at the concentration camp?

2. In what way was Jack's father's job at the camp considered to be a good one?

3. Why did Jack have to keep his potato hidden?

4. When did Jack truly appreciate the extent of his father's sacrifice?

5. What was the real meaning of the baked potato for the Sheradsky family?

6. Suppose Jack's father had kept his smuggled potatoes for himself. What would your opinion be of him?

7. It has been said that extreme hardship and suffering can change someone's personality. Will it make a person better or worse? Why?

TO BEGIN

Below is a scrambled list of important events in the story, "The Baked Potato." Put the events in the correct order in which they took place, looking back at the story if you find it necessary:

1. Potato becomes most important thing in Jack's life
2. Jack comes to appreciate what his father had done
3. Given starvation rations
4. Jack sacrifices for his own children
5. Sent to a concentration camp
6. No more potatoes
7. The boy gets a potato from his father

TO REMEMBER AND PUT INTO PRACTICE

The first rule of storytelling was given in Lesson One: tell what happened clearly and in logical order. As you reread "The Baked Potato," you will see that the seven highlights of Jack Sheradsky's story are told in chronological order. The story makes sense as it moves along from step to step. The author apparently knew where he was going before he started to write — and that is essential for any writer. You must always remember the point you are making, the reason for what you are writing.

THE OPENING LINES

The start of a story is very important. Since writers want their work to be read and appreciated, they must introduce their material in a way which interests — or hooks — their readers. Notice the start of the story in this lesson:

"A baked potato and a father's love. That's an unlikely combination — and yet to Jack Sheradsky it is very meaningful."

There's something catchy about that introduction. We want to know more about the unlikely pairing of a potato and a parent's affection. Before we know it, we are in the Nazi concentration camp in 1942, experiencing the hunger of Jack Sheradsky and his father.

Turn back to the opening lines in Lesson Two's continuation of the gun-in-the-desk story:

"Three weeks had passed since my first day at Filmore High School."

Is that a good start for the story? Why? Write a different opening line which you feel the author could have used and explain its merits.

To Do

Here are the opening lines of three other stories which appear later in this book:

1. New Yorker Arnold Johnson was about to be robbed. (Lesson 21)
2. Poor people often dream about ways to make huge sums of money. (Lesson 20)
3. When Rita D'Aversa got home from shopping at the A&P, she noticed that her son had closed his bedroom door, something that 16-year-old Jerry never did. (Lesson 18)

Which of these stories would you want to read first? Why?

Take any one and develop it into a three-paragraph story. Compare your attempt with the one you will find in that story.

Before undertaking this assignment, review the comments on three-paragraph essays which you will find before Question 4 of *Your Turn* in the previous story.

ADVERBS

Here are some adverbs from the story "The Baked Potato."

unlikely
yet
systematically
desperately
today

Adverbs are not so numerous as adjectives, but you can see that they lend style and flavor to your writing. As you study the adverb section in your Handbook (page 132), you will be fleshing out your writing power.

EXPANDING YOUR VOCABULARY

Choose the correct meaning for each of these words from "The Baked Potato."

1. the *brutal* work day   a) cruel   b) lengthy   c) numbing
2. he *deprived* himself   a) tormented   b) saved for   c) kept from having
3. too *frail* to work   a) conscientious   b) weak   c) chilled
4. the classical *gesture*   a) topic   b) theme   c) deed
5. an *insignificant* baked potato   a) of little importance   b) meaningful   c) wasteful
6. his "*luxury*" had been withdrawn   a) beyond what is really necessary   b) essential item   c) recreation
7. daily food *ration*   a) fixed allowance   b) supplement   c) intake
8. the life-*sustaining* potato   a) threatening   b) long   c) supporting
9. *systematically* working them to death   a) horribly   b) according to plan   c) viciously
10. *vivid* in Jack's mind   a) bright   b) startling   c) hazy

Lesson 7
CONCLUSIONS

READING PALMS IN INDIA

On a busy street in New Delhi, India, a young secretary was having her palm read during her lunch hour. The palmist was Rattan Kashinath Joshi, a 12-year-old who lives by his wits in the big city.

"Will I ever get married?" she asked.

Young Rattan scrutinized her hand intently. "You've already been married," he laughed. The woman blushed as she acknowledged the truth of that statement, while the onlookers applauded the wisdom of the young boy.

Later, Rattan explained to a reporter that he had noticed a lighter skin tone on the finger where the woman would have worn a marriage ring. Apparently she had removed the ring after her divorce. By being sharp-eyed and shrewd beyond his years, Rattan manages to survive in India, earning several dollars a day.

That afternoon he also informed a sailor of an upcoming sea voyage, predicted a raise in pay for a bank teller, told a pregnant woman to expect a baby girl, and cautioned a motorcyclist about a possible accident within the next three months.

Rattan learned his trade from an uncle. Although he claims to believe in palmistry, he readily admits that his knowledge of human nature and his lively patter are more important than anything he sees in a person's hand.

"If my client is over 60, I tell him that he has just recovered from a serious illness; if it's a young lady, I tell her about a handsome man who will come into her life shortly. Everyone goes away happy, and I get a big tip. It's like being in show business," Rattan confided.
"What do you see in your own palm?" the reporter asked.

Rattan looked down. "It needs to be washed," he said with a grin and disappeared into the huge crowd.

TIME TO REMEMBER AND REFLECT

1. How did the secretary try to trap young Rattan?

2. List two of the predictions which the clever palmist made for his customers during the afternoon.

3. What are two reasons for Rattan's success in the business of reading palms?

4. How did Rattan arrange to get big tips from his customers?

5. What evidence is there that Rattan did not believe too strongly in his ability to predict the future?

6. Suppose you were 12 years old and had to earn your living in a big city. What would you do?

7. Is it possible that the lines in your palm can indicate your future? Do you believe that an astrologist can tell you the truth about your personality or future based upon the day and month of your birth?

TYPES OF ENDINGS

Ho-Hum Endings

Have you ever ended a book report or essay in the following ways?
"Therefore, I recommend this novel to all teenagers who enjoy a good adventure story."
"For all the above reasons, I am opposed to the death penalty."
"Now you know how I spent my summer vacation."

Every year, thousands of teachers have groaned at those lines — not because the statements are irrelevant or technically in error, but because they are flat, stale, and boring. Being able to conclude a writing assignment in a stylish manner is a desirable skill, and you should take pains to acquire it. In the writing section of "The Baked Potato" lesson, we were concerned with the impact of a selection's opening lines. Now let us give some attention to signing off properly.

Humor

Several of this book's selections conclude in a light-hearted manner:

Leonard Stavisky, in "Doctor Shanna," Lesson 5, has his tongue in his cheek when he says, "I know Shanna [his dog] couldn't be a Ph.D. After all, she flunked out of obedience school."

After listing all the currently popular names for boys and girls, ("What's In a Name? Plenty!" Lesson 15) the writer's last words are, "What ever happened to Gizella Werberzerek Piffle?" By resurrecting that incredibly artificial name, he has provided a humorous twist that is an acceptable ending for that kind of article.

Although "Fearful of School," Lesson 14, is a serious piece, it ends with a joke which is pertinent to the theme of the article: "'I know how awful it (going to school) must be for you, Henry', she pleaded, 'but after all, you are the principal.'"

In "Reading Palms in India," we make the acquaintance of the likable Rattan, the 12-year-old showman who manages to live by his wits in New Delhi. The brief character sketch, which is enlivened by the boy's tricks of the trade, ends appropriately with a clever remark that we may remember long after the other details of the story have been forgotten:

"What do you see in your own palm?" the reporter asked.

Rattan looked down. "It needs to be washed," he said with a grin and disappeared into the huge crowd.

Show business comedies are supposed to "leave 'em laughing" — and that advice applies to some writing as well.

Foreshadowing

It is sometimes effective to conclude by just implying what is going to happen next, without actually spelling it all out. Foreshadowing of the type used in "A Mother's Decision," which you will find on page 63, works quite well:

"Give me the police," Mrs. D'Aversa said.

The major criticism of that ending is its popularity — countless movies and TV shows have faded out after those melodramatic words.

Summary...Plus

Leaving the reader with a general review of the theme of your work, plus a memorable tag line, is often commendable:

It was an expensive way for me to get an education, but I learned the terrible price of fear. ("The Gun in the Desk," Lesson 2)

He knew that with such a tradition, his own children would pass on their baked potatoes when the time came. ("The Baked Potato," Lesson 6)

Although he was Jewish and I am Catholic, I will always pray for him ("He Had a Mission in the World," Lesson 17)

Mr. Hawkins called it a woman's place to get coffee. I call that downright chauvinism. ("The Revolt of Helen," Lesson 30)

PARTING SHOTS

Here are the closing lines from some of the world's most famous pieces of writing. Read them, and see if you can explain why these endings have made such an indelible impression upon the reading public.

Peyton Farquhar was dead; his body, with a broken neck, swung gently from side to side beneath the timbers of the Owl Creek bridge. ("Occurrence at Owl Creek Bridge" by Ambrose Bierce)

"Oh! my poor Matilda! Mine (diamonds) were false. They were not worth over five hundred francs!" ("The Necklace" by Guy de Maupassant)

When we let freedom ring, when we let it ring from every village and every hamlet, from every state and every city, we will be able to speed up that day when all of God's children, black men and white men, Jews and Gentiles, Protestants and Catholics, will be able to join hands and sing in the words of that old Negro spiritual, "Free at last! Free at last! Thank God almighty, we are free at last." ("I Have a Dream" by Martin Luther King)

But of all the senses, I am sure that sight must be the most delightful. ("Three Days to See" by Helen Keller)

And so I leave it with all of you: Which came out of the opened door — the lady, or the tiger? ("The Lady or the Tiger" by Frank Stockton)

"Villains," I shrieked, "dissemble no more! I admit the deed! — tear up the planks! here, here! —it is the beating of his hideous heart!" ("The Tell-Tale Heart" by Edgar Allan Poe)

...and that government of the people, by the people, for the people, shall not perish from the earth. ("The Gettysburg Address" by Abraham Lincoln)

Then, with that faint, fleeting smile playing across his lips, he faced the firing squad; erect and motionless, proud and disdainful, Walter Mitty, the Undefeated, inscrutable to the last. ("The Secret Life of Walter Mitty" by James Thurber)

I profess, in the sincerity of my heart, that I have not the least personal interest in endeavoring to promote this necessary work, having no other motive than the public good of my country, by advancing our trade, providing for infants, relieving the poor, and giving some pleasure to the rich. I have no children by which I can propose to get a single penny; the youngest being nine years old, and my wife past child-bearing. ("A Modest Proposal" by Jonathan Swift)

A rift in the clouds in a gray day threw a shaft of sunlight upon her coffin as her nervous energetic little body sank to its last sleep. But the soul of her, the glowing, gorgeous, fervent soul of her, surely was flaming in eager joy upon some other dawn. ("Mary White" by William Allen White)

1. Which of the endings do you think seems most effective? Why?

2. Which of the endings could conceivably be the *opening* line of the work from which it came? Why?

PREPOSITIONS, CONJUNCTIONS

The following prepositions and conjunctions from Lesson Seven introduce you to the "cement" words that keep our blocks of ideas together.

Prepositions:
   on
   in
   during
   by
   of
   to
   after
   beyond
Conjunctions:
   while
   although
   if
   and

Work on the exercises on prepositions and conjunctions in the Handbook. It will help to round out your knowledge of the parts of speech.

EXPANDING YOUR VOCABULARY

Match the vocabulary words in Column A with the meanings in Column B.

A	B
1. acknowledged	a. very attentively
2. apparently	b. told the future
3. confided	c. seemingly
4. intently	d. admitted
5. palmistry	e. a salesperson's rapid speech
6. patter	f. examined carefully
7. predicted	g. told as a secret
8. readily	h. having a sharp mind
9. scrutinized	i. without hesitation
10. shrewd	j. telling fortunes by reading the lines on people's palms

Lesson 8
TOPIC SENTENCES

PINNED TO THE MAT

Richard Stoner is an all-around athlete. Outstanding in basketball, soccer, and karate, he was shocked when turned down for his high school wrestling team. The coach pointed out that it was not a matter of Richard's ability or desire. Rather, it was the school's concern for the boy's welfare which led them to bar him from the squad. Richard Stoner is blind in one eye, and the officials refused to jeopardize his sight by allowing the 15-year-old to compete in a fierce contact sport like wrestling.

Richard's parents had brought their son up to believe that even if his vision was not perfect, he was not really handicapped. From his early years on, he had been encouraged to take part in all physical activities despite the fact that he had only one good eye.

The Stoners were deeply upset over what they felt to be an act of prejudice. As Richard explained, "I would like very much to be treated like everyone else. It's unconstitutional to discriminate against someone who has a slight disability."

The president of the school board didn't want to come off as the villain of the piece. George Grim told a reporter, "Our position is that the school physician does not think that Richard should be allowed in contact sports; he bases that on guidelines in a medical journal."

The Stoners are aware of the risks. Nevertheless, they feel that the chances of Richard's other eye being damaged are slight. The greater risk, according to them, would be to Richard's normal development and to his attitude toward himself. "We are going to appeal to state and federal authorities," Richard's parents said.

How would you rule in this case?

TIME TO REMEMBER AND REFLECT

1. Why did the school refuse to allow Richard on the wrestling team?

2. In what other sports did Richard excel?

3. Why were Richard's parents upset over the school's decision?

28   4. What support did the school board's president have for his decision?

5. What was the next step for the Stoner family to take?

6. Were the school officials more concerned about Richard's health than his parents were? Explain.

7. Let us suppose that as the result of a wrestling accident, Richard's good eye was damaged. What comments might his parents make about such a tragedy?

8. How would you feel if you were assigned to wrestle against Richard in a schoolwide competition? How would you feel if you had injured him accidentally and caused serious damage to his other eye?

THE TOPIC SENTENCE

Taking one sentence from each of the five paragraphs in "Pinned to the Mat," we get the following story:

"Richard Stoner is blind in one eye and the officials refuse to jeopardize his sight by allowing the 15-year-old to compete in a fierce contact sport such as wrestling. Richard's parents had brought their son up to believe that although his vision was impaired, he was not handicapped. The Stoners were deeply upset over what they felt to be an act of prejudice. The president of the school board didn't want to come off as the villain of the piece. 'We are going to appeal to state and federal authorities,' Richard's parents said."

As you can see, the story is condensed but it still makes good sense. The reason is that we were presented with the key or *topic sentence* from each paragraph. It is generally possible to examine any paragraph from a cohesive piece of writing and to identify the topic sentence — the one which states the main idea of the paragraph.

In a sense, those topic sentences are the bare bones of each paragraph, waiting to be fleshed out in sentences which explain, clarify, add to, expand upon, or justify the topic sentence. When you sharpen your skills as a writer, you will automatically spin out those topic sentences as you plan your work and then develop them as you carry out the task of writing.

Where Should the Topic Sentence Be Placed?

In "Pinned to the Mat," the topic sentences are the last sentences in two of the five paragraphs. More commonly they are placed at the start of the paragraph, but there is no hard and fast rule about it.

The following paragraph is from "Why So Late?" in Lesson Four. Find the sentence which serves as the topic sentence.

> Psychologists say that lateness rarely is an accident. More likely it is connected to unconscious feelings about school or your job. You may be bored, and lateness is your way of expressing your resistance to wasting your time. Or, since you feel insecure because of poor achievement, lateness is your way of saying "no" to an unhappy situation. Then again, you may resent authority. You want to feel free, unhampered by rules, regulations, bells, time clocks, and I.D. cards. That could account for your tardiness.

Could the first sentence, the topic sentence of this paragraph, have been used at the close of the paragraph? Any advantage? Would it still be considered the topic sentence? The answer is yes.

The next paragraph is from "Doctor Shanna," Lesson Five. Find the topic sentence of this paragraph.

> Almost all of the colleges in this country can be regarded as respectable institutions. In return for tuition money they offer a variety of useful courses and, ultimately, a degree for those who qualify. There are a few colleges, however, which operate in a shady manner, providing degrees to which people are not entitled, for courses which they never took. One of the most notorious in recent years was Pacific College in Los Angeles, California.

The first sentence doesn't give you the gist of the paragraph but the third sentence does. That is the topic sentence, of course, and it can come in the middle of the paragraph.

YOUR TURN

A. Write a paragraph of approximately 50-75 words using one of the following as your topic sentence. Place the topic sentence at the *start* of the paragraph.

  1. It's impossible to run for a major political office in this country unless you can raise huge sums of money.
  2. Television news programs are good, but they can't take the place of daily newspapers.
  3. Sometimes teachers teach more than they realize.

B. Write a paragraph of approximately 50-75 words using one of the following as your topic sentence. This time, place the topic sentence at the *end* of the paragraph.

  1. If it were up to me, all high school courses would be pass/fail with no numerical marks given.
  2. I'll have to admit that crime does not pay.
  3. In this contest, there was no winner.

EXPANDING YOUR VOCABULARY

Choose the correct meaning for the words in italics.

  1. *appeal* to authorities   a) to ask for a decision   b) salute   c) refuse to deal with
  2. a fierce *contact* sport   a) competitive   b) tiring   c) touching physically
  3. *despite* the fact   a) in addition to   b) since   c) even though
  4. *guidelines* in a medical journal   a) regulations   b) articles   c) summaries
  5. he was not *handicapped*   a) at a disadvantage   b) threatened   c) defeated
  6. vision was *impaired*   a) made worse   b) fixed   c) operated upon
  7. *jeopardize* his sight   a) place in danger   b) cancel   c) reform
  8. outstanding in *karate*   a) international sports   b) method of fighting   c) wrestling
  9. aware of the *risks*   a) compensation   b) dangers   c) chances
  10. concern for the boy's *welfare*   a) health and happiness   b) performance   c) progress

Lesson 9
DEVELOPING TOPIC SENTENCES

TESTS THAT REALLY COUNT

The school and state exams you may be taking this year are important, of course, but not nearly as critical to your future as those which Chinese high school seniors face each July. Those who pass can look forward to high level careers as engineers, scientists, and diplomats. Those who fail, however, will probably spend the rest of their lives on farms or in lowly factory jobs.

Anyone who has ever been jittery about an exam in this country can imagine the terrible tension which exists among Chinese teenagers each summer. In the U.S. we have room in our universities for 40 percent of all high school graduates. But in China, only 4 percent of the college-age students can be admitted. As a result, the competition is unusually fierce, the stakes are unusually high. Nervous breakdowns are fairly common among students who cannot take the pressure put upon them by anxious parents.

The 12½ hours of tests are spread over three days and administered in six subjects: math, Chinese literature, a foreign language, and politics are taken by all candidates; liberal arts majors must also pass history and geography, while science majors have to get by physics and chemistry. None of the questions are easy.

Because so much is riding on the outcome of the tests, most pupils spend a year or more in special coaching courses that help to prepare them for the brutal ordeal. It also helps to be politically conscious. Last year's essay question, for example, was "Why do we have to strengthen the leadership of the Communist Party?"

Government leaders are deeply concerned about the problems to which these highly selective tests have given rise. On one hand, they view the tests as necessary to develop the intellectual talent their nation will need in the coming decades. On the other, they do not want hundreds of thousands of young Chinese to become frustrated by failure.

"Working in a factory is not such a terrible alternative," said Li Wang of the Department of Education in Peking.

"If that is the case," a high school senior was heard to comment, "Mr. Li can take over my father's machine in the shoe factory tomorrow."

TIME TO REMEMBER AND REFLECT

1. According to the article, what are some of the jobs available to Chinese college graduates?

2. What percentage of U.S. high school graduates find places in our universities?

3. What subjects are the Chinese students tested in? How long do the tests take?

4. Why do the Chinese government leaders continue to sponsor such difficult tests?

5. What evidence is there to show that high school seniors take the tests very seriously?

6. What could the Chinese government do to ease the pressure on high school graduates? Why don't they do it?

7. "The Chinese are no fools," a businessman remarked. "They are not going to fritter away money on just any ignoramus who wants to go to college the way we in the U.S. do." What is your opinion of that statement?

BEYOND THE TOPIC SENTENCE

A reading of an article's topic sentence should provide a useful summary of its contents. But although the topic sentences lend structure to a writing selection, they must be fleshed out properly if the article is to have coherence and substance. That development can take place in a number of ways. Let us examine "Tests That Really Count" to see how some of its topic sentences were developed.

Explanation

The school and state exams you may be taking this year are important, of course, but not nearly as critical to your future as those which Chinese high school seniors face each July.

We would expect this topic sentence to be followed by an explanation of the tremendous importance of those exams for Chinese teenagers, and it is:

Those who pass can look forward to high level careers as engineers, scientists, and diplomats. Those who fail, however, will probably spend the rest of their lives on farms or in lowly factory jobs.

Contrast

Anyone who has ever been jittery about an exam in this country can imagine the terrible tension which exists among Chinese teenagers each summer.

This topic sentence is followed by an explanation of the difference between our two countries in the area of college admissions and the reason for the great tension among Chinese students:

In the U.S. we have room in our universities for 40 percent of all high school graduates. But in China, only 4 percent of their college-age students can be admitted. As a result, the competition is unusually fierce, the stakes are unusually high. Nervous breakdowns are fairly common among students who cannot take the pressure put upon them by anxious parents.

Details

Government leaders are deeply concerned about the problems which these highly selective tests have given rise to.

Here, we expect more detail about exactly what worries the government leaders:

> On one hand, they view the tests as necessary to develop the intellectual talent their nation will need in the coming decades. On the other, they do not want hundreds of thousands of young Chinese to become frustrated by failure.

Such orderly paragraph development shows us that the article was constructed carefully. When you write, you should be able to review your paragraphs in similar fashion, to see if you developed your topic sentences appropriately.

WAYS TO DEVELOP TOPIC SENTENCES

You can develop or support your topic sentences with:

Reasons

In "Why So Late?" Lesson 4, the opening topic sentence is

> Psychologists say that lateness rarely is an accident.

The paragraph goes on to offer a number of reasons to explain that statement: lateness is connected to unconscious feelings about school or job, boredom, way of expressing resistance, resentment of authority, etc.

Incidents, Anecdotes

In "Outside the Law," Lesson 26, the final topic sentence is:

> In their search for quick justice, the White Hand representatives have committed serious injustices, their critics complain.

The rest of the paragraph relates an incident that illustrates this topic sentence:

> An innocent house painter opened his door to explain to a White Hand team that the thief they were seeking did not live in his house — but he was cut down by a staccato blast of gun fire before he could tell his story.

Facts, Statistics

The lead topic sentence in "A Family Drama," Lesson 13, identifies aplastic anemia as a killing disease:

> Among the fatal diseases which plague mankind is aplastic anemia.

The writer then presents the facts to support that statement:

> The normally red bone marrow of the patient becomes fatty and yellow and fails to form enough of its vital cellular products. The lack of bone marrow white cells and platelets in the blood is characteristic of the disease. A lack of platelets can lead to bleeding — which spells death when it occurs in the brain. Unless the process invading the marrow can be suppressed, the person who contracts aplastic anemia is surely doomed.

Being able to expand upon a topic sentence with facts and statistics shows that you know what you are talking about.

SUMMARIZING

The spine of your article is made up of its topic sentences. But unless you follow them up with *reasons*, *incidents*, and *facts*, you will have only a frail skeleton of an argument instead of a solidly constructed specimen.

Note, for example, how weak the above paragraph would have been if the writer had merely repeated his topic sentence without adding the facts:

> Among the fatal diseases which plague mankind is aplastic anemia. If you get it, your days are numbered. Generally, little hope is held out for the victims of aplastic anemia. The body becomes weaker and weaker; ultimately, there is nothing that can be done to prolong the patient's life. Untreated, aplastic anemia is a cruel killer.

YOUR TURN

A. Select *three* of the topic sentences below. Use reasons, incidents, or facts to develop them into effective paragraphs:

1. Although many adults, especially teachers, knock television, I have found it to be an important part of my education.
2. Quick thinking can save lives.
3. Our Thanksgiving dinner was one of the greatest feasts of all times.
4. "Neither a borrower nor a lender be" was good advice from Polonius and my father.
5. Most people like to travel, but there's a good deal to see right here at home.
6. Sometimes the truth can hurt.

B. Analyze the following paragraphs, telling which techniques the writers used to develop their topic sentences:

> Calvin Coolidge, our thirtieth president, was named "Silent Cal" by reporters because of his brevity of speech. He tried to get by with one word when a dozen words might have been required. One Sunday, after Mr. Coolidge had listened to an interminable sermon, a group of newsmen gathered around him outside the church. One reporter asked: "We know that the sermon was on the topic of sin. What did the minister say?" "He was against it," Coolidge replied.

> There are any number of people who try to find more respectable or glamorous titles for the ordinary jobs they hold. My uncle calls himself a sanitary engineer — but he's really a garbage collector. Our neighbor always lists "transportation executive" on his employment applications, but I know that he's a taxi driver. Funeral directors are "morticians," bookies are "investment counselors," and typists are "Gal Fridays."

> Dr. Thomas Dooley, one of the truly outstanding people of our century, deserves to be better known for his humanitarian efforts. In the 1950s he led a mission to treat a half-million starving Vietnamese refugees. He was faced with enormous handicaps such as the lack of funds and official support, ignorance, prejudice, disease, and a debilitating cancer which eventually took his life. The organization he founded, MEDICO, brought medical aid, comfort, and hope to the world's sick and needy.

SUBORDINATE CLAUSES

which Chinese high school seniors face each July
who pass
while science majors have to get by physics and chemistry
because so much is riding on the outcome of the tests
if one is politically conscious

These excerpts, which were taken from Lesson Nine, illustrate the use of subordinate clauses in a good piece of writing. How monotonous it would be to read a story which contains only simple or compound sentences! It would not show the emphasis the more important ideas deserve. You can learn more about subordinate clauses by referring to the Handbook (page 156).

EXPANDING YOUR VOCABULARY

Match the vocabulary words in Column A with the correct meanings in Column B.

A		B	
1.	alternative (n)	a.	nervous condition
2.	anxious	b.	nervous
3.	candidate	c.	savage
4.	decade	d.	showing intelligence
5.	fierce	e.	one who studies for a degree
6.	frustrated	f.	period of ten years
7.	intellectual	g.	prevented from doing something
8.	jittery	h.	prizes; things to gain
9.	stakes	i.	a choice
10.	tension	j.	troubled; worried; uneasy

Lesson 10
STACKING THE CARDS

PLAY BALL?

The Harwood Athletic Association Little League teams stood tall on the baseball field, ready to march in the Opening Day Parade. Their clean and pressed uniforms presented a colorful spectacle to the onlookers who were gathered to cheer for the young players.

On the sidelines, however, their faces stained with tears, were 12-year-old twin brothers, Allen and Paul Bukowsky. The boys' uniforms had been confiscated and the twins barred from competition because of a League rule which made their father fighting mad.

It seems that the Harwood Athletic Association requires each player to sell 96 candy bars as part of the fund raising campaign. When the Bukowsky boys returned most of the candy unsold, they were marked ineligible for the baseball season. It broke their hearts.

Fred Gendler, Harwood's president, puffed on his cigar as he justified the Association's action: "Without that money we couldn't run our schedule; we couldn't offer the kids the high level of team play which this community is accustomed to. If a parent wants his child to get something out of Little League, he has to put something into it."

"It's insane to penalize kids for something like this," responded Mr. Bukowsky. "I paid a registration fee and offered to serve as a volunteer umpire but Gendler sneered at that, saying it was no substitute for the candy sale. What should I do? Be blackmailed for $76 worth of chocolate? It's unfair, and I'm not going to let them get away with it."

Mr. Bukowsky is backing up his threat with legal action. He filed suit against Harwood, asking for $15,000 in damages and a temporary restraining order. Although the judge denied the order (which would have held up the start of the season), he left the damage portion of the suit on the court calendar.

"I never thought our League would be that way," young Paul muttered. "My brother and I wouldn't want to play now even if they let us."

"Some sportsmanship!" added their father. "I can't believe that the great American pastime has to rely on chocolate bars for its success."

TIME TO REMEMBER AND REFLECT

1. What made Mr. Bukowsky fighting mad?

2. What evidence is there that the twins made some attempt to sell the candy bars?

3. What contributions had Mr. Bukowsky already made to the Harwood Athletic Association?

4. What did Mr. Bukowsky want the courts to do?

5. How can we measure the anger of young Paul Bukowsky?

6. "Big deal!" a neighbor said. "Why doesn't Bukowsky just sell the candy the way the rest of us do and not make such a big fuss about it?" Tell why you agree or disagree with that statement.

7. One of the frequent criticisms of Little Leagues over the years is that the adults get too involved and spoil the kids' fun. From your experience, are those criticisms valid?

WORD POWER

We have heard that the pen is mightier than the sword — and, by extension, the typewriter is more powerful than the cannon. The more we learn, the more we come to realize that people who use words cleverly have a formidable weapon at their command.

Words are often used to influence opinion. In a political campaign, one candidate is praised while his opponent is sliced up like a salami. Advertisers use words to sell cosmetics, bankers use words to lure depositors, and governments use words to publicize their successes or cover up their failures.

All of that is understandable. But in an ordinary news story we do not expect the reporter to be taking sides. However, it does happen, and as readers and writers we need to be alert to such stacking of the cards.

STACKING THE CARDS

Let's examine "Play Ball?" for evidence of partiality by the reporter. On the surface it is a story about a controversy. Will Mr. Bukowsky win in the courts or was Mr. Gendler right in enforcing the Harwood Athletic Association's rule for Little League participation? On the one hand, we are presented with the plight of the young boys and their irate father; on the other, there is the seemingly reasonable argument of the League's president, telling us that his organization needs money if it is to carry out its good work for the community's children.

But has the author been fair in his presentation of the problem? Are both sides given equal treatment, or does the reporter's prejudice show? Has he stacked the cards in this local drama? Your clues lie in phrases and sentences like these:

[The twins'] faces stained with tears

The boys' uniforms had been confiscated and the twins barred from competition...

They were marked ineligible for the baseball season.

It broke their hearts.

Fred Gendler, Harwood's president, puffed on his cigar...

Gendler sneered at that...

My brother and I wouldn't want to play now even if they let us.

Some sportsmanship!

...great American pastime has to rely on chocolate bars for its success.

We must admit that the Bukowskys' case has been presented in a manner to prejudice us in their favor. Putting those tear-stained little boys up against a cigar-chewing executive who "sneers" at an honest offer is not exactly playing fair.

In analyzing writing, we should note the use of words intended to mold our opinion. When we are told that a person "strode" into the room, we get a more positive image than if he is described as "ambling" or "shuffling" into the room. A witness can be portrayed as responding "forcefully" and "directly" or "mumbling apologetically."

Can you tell when the cards are stacked? It's important to know.

YOUR TURN

A. Rewrite "Play Ball?" so that Mr. Gendler's viewpoint is pictured in a more sympathetic light. The problem facing you is how to switch the emphasis away from the tear-stained twins and their outraged parent.

B. Several of the stories in this book invite you to render a personal decision on a controversial matter: Should a mother turn her son in to the police, Lesson 18; should a member of the Ku Klux Klan be given his high school diploma, Lesson 11; and should a man risk his life in order to help a dying relative, Lesson 13?

Take one of these problems and develop it into a short selection which favors one point over the other. For example, you might stack the cards so that the reader does not want the mother to turn her son in to the police.

C. Read your daily newspaper carefully in order to discover an article in which opinion could be influenced by a reporter's slanting of a controversial issue. Bring it to class along with your analysis of how the reporter attempted to accomplish his aim.

PHRASES

on the baseball field
to cheer for the young players
barred from competition
to rely on chocolate bars for its success

These expressions from Lesson Ten demonstrate the important function performed by phrases. It proves once again that effective writing requires an understanding of the basic structure of the language. Study the section on phrases in the Handbook and see how your writing will improve when you apply this knowledge to good purpose.

EXPANDING YOUR VOCABULARY

Choose the correct meaning for the word in italics.

1. the twins had been *barred*   a) attacked b) forbidden c) treated badly
2. should I be *blackmailed*   a) threatened b) punished c) disqualified
3. fund raising *campaign*   a) party b) excursion c) planned course of action
4. barred from *competition*   a) organized games b) trial c) races
5. uniforms had been *confiscated*   a) torn b) taken away c) packed
6. they were marked *ineligible*   a) illegal b) not ready c) unfit
7. he *justified* the action   a) gave a good reason for b) judged c) ruled upon
8. to *penalize* kids   a) demote b) punish c) instruct
9. a colorful *spectacle*   a) noteworthy sight b) program c) banner
10. a *temporary* order   a) comprehensive b) partial c) for the time being

Lesson 11
REPETITION

THE KLANSMAN AND THE DIPLOMA

"They are in for a fight," declared Aaron Morrison, "if they try to violate my right of free expression."

The 17-year-old Morrison, a teenage organizer for the Ku Klux Klan, was talking heatedly about his school's decision to deny him a diploma.

Reverend Thomas Ploude, principal of Holy Spirit High School in Absecon, New Jersey, had said, "Aaron's Klan activities are totally against our teachings. I will send a record of his grades to any college which requests it, but I absolutely refuse to issue him a diploma."

"They are in for a fight," repeated Aaron Morrison, "if they try to violate my right of free expression."

The American Civil Liberties Union is opposed to the racist policies and philosophy of the Ku Klux Klan. Nevertheless, they are supporting Morrison in his complaint against the school authorities. A spokesman for the A.C.L.U. called the matter "a clear violation of Morrison's constitutional rights."

School officials pointed out that the awarding of a diploma not only signifies that a student has been successful in his studies, but it also indicates that he has given evidence of good citizenship. An assistant principal commented, "Morrison's marks are not being disputed; but if we are to maintain the respect of the academic community we must also take his Klan activities into consideration."

Aaron Morrison has vowed to go "to the highest court in the land" in order to compel Holy Spirit High to grant him a diploma.

"I earned it," said the fiery young man, "and I am certain that the courts will see it my way."

"It's ironic that Aaron keeps referring to the law and the Constitution of the United States," remarked a history teacher at the school, "because his own KKK has often broken the law throughout the last 150 years."

"They are in for a fight," Aaron Morrison reminded the reporters, "if they try to violate my right of free expression."

TIME TO REMEMBER AND REFLECT

1. Why would the American Civil Liberties Union normally be opposed to members of the Ku Klux Klan?

2. Why is the American Civil Liberties Union willing to support Aaron Morrison's case?

3. On what grounds did the school refuse to give the young Klansman his diploma?

4. What did Morrison's principal say that he would do to help the young man?

5. Why did a history teacher think it was ironic for Morrison to fall back on the law and the U.S. Constitution?

6. Aaron Morrison must have been very impressed with his right to free expression because he referred to it over and over again. Can you think of any situation in which free expression should not be permitted?

7. The American Civil Liberties Union has often gone to court to protect a citizen's constitutional rights. Should they come to the defense of a journalist who was arrested for publishing a hate sheet filled with prejudice toward minority groups?

USING REPETITION FOR EFFECT

English teachers are often quick to advise their students to "avoid repetition." They would do better to say, "avoid *needless* repetition" — because repetition with a purpose can be an excellent technique for a writer or speaker.

In Shakespeare's *Julius Caesar,* Marc Antony uses the word "honourable" ten times during his funeral oration in Act III, Scene 2. Since Shakespeare had an extensive vocabulary, it is obvious that he could have found a variety of synonyms for that word rather than repeat it so often. But Shakespeare's purpose is quite clear; after the first two uses of "honourable," the audience is well aware of Marc Antony's relentless irony in employing that word over and over again.

Similarly, in *Othello,* Shakespeare makes frequent use of the adjective "honest" to describe Iago, one of the most *dishonest* characters in all literature. The repetition is for effect, and it is brilliantly effective.

In the same play, Iago uses repetition himself ("put money in thy purse") as he deals with the young dupe, Roderigo. Cyrano de Bergerac, Edmond Rostand's witty master of language, also entertains us with "I shall thrust as I end the refrain" — repeating that line regularly as he duels with the Vicomte and then skewering that nobleman at the final repetition.

When the Englishman Robert Southey (1774-1843) wrote his satiric poem, "The Battle of Blenheim," he, too, turned to repetition in order to hammer home his thesis about the futility of war:

> But what they fought each other for
> I could not well make out
> "But everybody said," quoth he
> "That 'twas a famous victory."

In short, good writers are inventive enough to avoid needless repetition but clever enough to use repetition to good advantage. In the selection you just read, Aaron Morrison's statement, "They are in for a fight if they try to violate my right of free expression" was repeated to impress the reader with the firmness of Morrison's resolve. Appearing at the start, middle, and end of the article, it helps to convince you that Morrison means business. Of course, he might be repeating that line to bolster up his own courage (the gentleman doth protest too much), but we don't know enough about him to jump to that conclusion.

YOUR TURN

A. Write a three-paragraph composition, about 200 words long, in which you repeat a word, phrase, or sentence in order to emphasize a point. It could be for comic or ironic effect.

B. Use the phrase "but nobody would listen to me" several times in a poem or composition.

C. Read "When I Was One and Twenty" by A.E. Housman and "Boots" by Rudyard Kipling to see how poets make use of repetition. In a paragraph, explain the different purposes of both poets.

EXPANDING YOUR VOCABULARY

Match each word in Column A with the correct meaning in Column B.

A	B
1. community	a. refuse to give
2. compel	b. quarreled about; debated
3. deny	c. principles which people believe in
4. disputed	d. to force
5. fiery	e. disturb; interfere with
6. ironic	f. belief that one race is superior to another
7. philosophy	g. full of feeling; excitable
8. racist	h. expressing one thing and meaning another
9. violate	i. people with similar interests
10. vowed	j. promised

Lesson 12
USING QUOTATIONS

THE DYNAMIC REVEREND JESSE JACKSON

"If a young man or a woman goes to any state university in this country for four years, it will cost less than $20,000. But if he or she goes to the state penitentiary for four years, it will cost over $50,000."

With impressive statements such as that, the Reverend Jesse Jackson has been calling the public's attention to the need for moral, social, educational, and economic reforms. As a presidential candidate, and one of the most dynamic speakers in our country, Jesse Jackson commands an audience's respect not only for his style but for the power of the messages which he delivers so eloquently. A number of school systems have invited him to address their students, knowing that his motivational techniques are often far more effective than those used by the teachers.

Recently, Rev. Jackson left these thoughts with pupils in Chicago:

What does it matter if we have a new book or an old book, if we open neither?

You must know that it's not your *aptitude* but your *attitude* which will determine your *altitude*.

Both tears and sweat are wet and salty, but they render a different result. Tears will get you sympathy, but sweat will get you change.

A number of years ago, few school administrators or establishment officials would have dreamed of inviting Jesse Jackson to an assembly program. He was too radical, too abrasive, too much of a threat to law and order, they might have thought. Today, however, they seek him out eagerly and praise his constructive qualities.

Why is Jesse Jackson such a hit with young audiences? To start with, he is handsome and speaks with the skill of a trained Baptist minister. For another, he tells it "the way it is," using language which the listeners rarely hear from a school platform. But the real reasons for the success of this charismatic preacher are the potent ideas which he communicates.

"I'll never forget Mr. Jackson's words at our graduation," said an 18-year-old from Atlanta:

"If we sow short-term pleasure, we will reap long-term pain. But if we sow short-term pain, we will reap long-term pleasure."

TIME TO REMEMBER AND REFLECT

1. Why did Jesse Jackson bring up the comparison between university and penitentiary costs?

2. Why are school systems now eager to hire Rev. Jackson to address their students? Why would they have been unwilling to do so a few years ago?

3. According to the article, why is Jesse Jackson so successful in dealing with teenagers?

4. What point did Rev. Jackson make about aptitude, attitude, and altitude?

5. One thing which Rev. Jackson says that our society needs is *moral* reform. What other kinds of reform is he seeking?

6. A skeptic said, "Jesse gets the kids all fired up when he speaks to them — but then they have to go out to face the same mess. So what's the use?" How would you answer that person?

7. Apparently many young people have been moved to help themselves by Rev. Jackson's words. Tell about someone who influenced you to do something worthwhile.

IN THE WORDS OF . . .

Sometimes the most effective way to report a story is with quotations. The readers get the flavor of the event by seeing the exact words of the participants. It helps, of course, if the speakers have some flair for oral expression. In the case of Reverend Jesse Jackson, we have the ideal candidate for a quotation-filled article since he is such a gifted phrasemaker.

The article you just read opens with an eye-catching pronouncement:

> If a young man or a woman goes to any state university in this country for four years, it will cost less than $20,000. But if he or she goes to the state penitentiary for four years, it will cost over $50,000.

Obviously, it was a good idea to introduce the selection with that provocative statement because most readers would like to hear more on that topic. It is a worthwhile technique to copy, assuming that you can lead off with an interesting quotation.

Quotable Quotes

In the middle of the article are three more memorable quotations:

> What does it matter if we have a new book or an old book, if we open neither?

> You must know that it's not your *aptitude* but your *attitude* which will determine your *altitude*.

> Both tears and sweat are wet and salty, but they render a different result. Tears will get you sympathy, but sweat will get you change.

These quotations help to reinforce the point that Reverend Jackson knows how to motivate an audience by providing them with choice morsels for thought. Merely saying, "Rev. Jackson made an indelible impression on the audience with his clever selection of words," would not have conveyed the power we find in the reported quotations.

The article concludes with another excerpt from Jesse Jackson's message:

> If we sow short-term pleasure, we will reap long-term pain. But if we sow short-term pain, we will reap long-term pleasure.

43

Using that quotation at the end of the selection lends balance to the organization of the piece. Reverend Jackson is an uncommonly talented orator, but even quotations from less gifted speakers can help to make an article more effective.

YOUR TURN

A. Take the following quotations from "The Dynamic Rev. Jesse Jackson" and, in a paragraph for each, explain its meaning. When you are through, ask a friend to read both and decide which is more expressive.

You must know that it's not your *aptitude* but your *attitude* which will determine your *altitude*.

If we sow short-term pleasure, we will reap long-term pain. But if we sow short-term pain, we will reap long-term pleasure.

B. Use the following quotations in a short composition/essay:

1. "Knowledge is power." —Francis Bacon
2. "Knowledge is the antidote to fear." —Ralph Waldo Emerson
3. "The first and wisest of them all professed To know this only, that he nothing knew." — John Milton

C. Below are six quotations taken from the works of the 19th century English writer, Oscar Wilde. Integrate at least *two* of them into a short composition/essay:

1. "It is always a silly thing to give advice, but to give good advice is absolutely fatal."
2. "A cynic is a man who knows the price of everything and the value of nothing."
3. "Duty is what one expects from others."
4. "Experience is the name everyone gives to their mistakes."
5. "Laughter is not at all a bad beginning for a friendship, and it is far the best ending for one."
6. "Moderation is a fatal thing. Nothing succeeds like excess."

EXPANDING YOUR VOCABULARY

Choose the correct meaning for the word in italics.

1. he was too *abrasive*   a) insincere b) harsh c) demanding
2. *aptitude* will determine your altitude   a) skill b) power of reasoning c) luck
3. this *charismatic* preacher   a) having great personal appeal b) religious c) highly trained
4. delivers so *eloquently*   a) poetically b) expressively c) reasonably
5. *impressive* statements   a) argumentative b) worth remembering c) decisive
6. *motivational* techniques   a) inspirational b) proven c) rehearsed
7. the state *penitentiary*   a) compound b) reservation c) jail
8. to *ponder* over   a) to think about b) to act upon c) to reject
9. *potent* ideas   a) insignificant b) powerful c) simple
10. he was too *radical*   a) behind the times b) extreme c) thoughtless

Lesson 13
FIGURES OF SPEECH

A FAMILY DRAMA

Among the fatal diseases which plague mankind is aplastic anemia. The normally red bone marrow of the patient becomes fatty and yellow and fails to form enough of its vital cellular products. The lack of bone marrow white cells and platelets in the blood is characteristic of the disease. A lack of platelets can lead to bleeding, which spells death when it occurs in the brain. Unless the process invading the marrow can be suppressed, the person who contracts aplastic anemia is surely doomed.

In recent years, considerable progress has been made in fighting the dread disease. Doctors have achieved success with the help of bone marrow transplants from family donors or people whose bone marrow is compatible. The match-ups have to be fairly exact otherwise the body rejects the transplant as an unwelcome guest.

That brings us to the distressing story of Phil McCoy of Fort Worth, Texas. When his doctors discovered that Phil had aplastic anemia, they tested the available relatives to find a likely donor. Phil's cousin, Terence Coyle, was found to have the ideal bone marrow for a successful transplant. Needless to say, Phil McCoy was overjoyed with the laboratory report. He and Terry had been as close as two coats of paint, and Phil knew he could rely on his cousin, a 250-pound, good-natured Santa Claus of a man.

Before the doctors could schedule the life-saving procedure, however, Coyle took his chips out of the pot. He said that he was sympathetic, to be sure, but because of his own recent health problems he could not agree to help his dying cousin. Phil McCoy felt lower than a cobra's belly when he heard the unexpected news.

McCoy's lawyer took the unusual step of asking the court to order Coyle to donate his bone marrow. Last week, Judge Jack Vickrey ruled against McCoy: "In our law, no one is obliged to jump into the water to save a drowning man." The judge went on to say, "Each individual's rights must be respected."

"I thought my cousin and I were like Damon and Pythias," McCoy said, "but there's nothing further I can do about it in the courts. Terry has some fear of dying during the transplant, and I can't get him to see that there's very little danger to him. I'm persistent, however, and hope that my prayers will get that Rock of Gibraltar to change his mind. His heart is really as big as this Lone Star state, and I feel that he won't let me down."

"Don't be too quick to condemn Coyle," his lawyer told the reporters. "You don't know how you might act if you were wearing his britches."

TIME TO REMEMBER AND REFLECT

1. What harmful effect does aplastic anemia have on the body?

2. Why was Phil surprised when Terry refused to donate his blood marrow?

3. On what grounds did the judge rule against Phil McCoy?

4. Why couldn't Phil advertise for a donor and offer to pay him?

5. What was the message that Terry Coyle's lawyer left with the reporters?

6. How would you act if you were in Terence Coyle's shoes? Would you be willing to undergo the marrow transplant?

7. Pretend that you are Phil McCoy, appealing to your cousin Terence. What could you say that might convince him to help you?

USING FIGURATIVE LANGUAGE

Generally, the simplest language is the most effective language:

> We have our doubts about this year's Yankee team. Many of the players are old or injured, and it is hard to see how they can make it through the season.

Similes and Metaphors

While this two-sentence paragraph is simple and effective, it does not mean that writers should shrink from using colorful words and expressions which add punch to their sentences. It is possible to convey the same information about the Yankees by means of figures of speech:

> We have our doubts about this year's Yankee team. Since their players are as old as the hills or as bandaged as Egyptian mummies, it is hard to see how they can make it through the heat of the summer.

This paragraph contains two figures of speech ("old as the hills" and "bandaged as Egyptian mummies") which are *similes*. A simile is a comparison between essentially different things, using *as* or *like* as connectives.

Although those two similes are attempts at livelier writing, they would be so much more successful if they weren't so trite, so hackneyed, so overworked. Here is another way of conveying the same thought about the New York baseball team:

> One would have to be Nostradamus to know where the Yankees will finish this year. Many of their players are overage destroyers or victims of the charge up San Juan Hill. They'll probably photo-finish, tongues hanging out, with Jack London's Buck.

This paragraph contains four figures of speech (Nostradamus, overage destroyers, San Juan Hill, Jack London's Buck) which are *metaphors*. A metaphor is a suggested comparison of dissimilar things *without* the use of *as* or *like*. The Yankees are not *like* overage destroyers — they *are* overage destroyers.

Granted, some creativity has gone into the above paragraph, but its strength depends upon the reader's knowing about Nostradamus, overage destroyers of World War II, the charge up San Juan Hill during the Spanish-American War, and Buck of *The Call of the Wild*. The whole point of figurative language is to create more vivid pictures for the reader, to communicate more clearly what you mean. Therefore, you must be sure that your readers will know what you are talking about when you use figures of speech.

Is this final paragraph an improvement over the others? Be prepared to tell why.

> This year's Yankee team is a squirming question mark. Their players are either old enough to remember gasoline at 35 cents a gallon, or they are as bandaged as Alan Alda's *M*A*S*H* patients. It's hard to see how those walking-wounded candidates for Social Security can survive the radar ovens of July and August.

Naturally, some writers are better than others when it comes to coining fresh comparisons. Their imaginative similes and metaphors enable us to see with greater clarity, to feel with greater pleasure. While we cannot hope to match those original talents, all of us can improve our abilities to communicate by practicing the use of figurative language and trading in our cliches for fresher words and phrases.

Literal-Figurative

When a writer uses a literal expression, he is relying completely on facts; when he uses a figurative expression, he is relying on imagination. It is literal to describe some Yankee players as "injured," but it is figurative to call them "battle casualties." In this case, using the figurative language makes the injuries sound serious, and suggests that they happened during an important struggle.

How would you express the following figures of speech in literal language?

Similes

1. high as an elephant's eye
2. silent as the tomb
3. chattering like a wilderness of monkeys
4. strong as a tower of Jello

Metaphors

1. I drifted into the *rapids* of traffic
2. Good news sends her *into orbit*
3. My report card *swaggered* across the desk
4. The sky *is a blackboard* high above us

Try Your Hand

Complete the following similes, using vivid expressions.

1. The workers leaving the factory looked like...
2. The pool was as crowded as...
3. To taste her apple pie was like...
4. The prizefighter's ears were like...
5. The gold coins shone like...
6. Her temper was as fiery as...
7. Listening to the boring lecture was like...
8. The horse's front legs snapped like...
9. The lightning was as jagged as...
10. Her voice was as melodious as...

Figurative Language in "A Family Drama"

rejects it as an unwelcome guest
close as two coats of paint
250-pound, good-natured Santa Claus of a man
took his chips out of the pot
lower than a cobra's belly

jump into the water to save a drowning man
like Damon and Pythias
that Rock of Gibraltar
big as the Lone Star state
wearing his britches

Take each of these ten expressions and explain the author's purpose in using it. Which are similes? Metaphors? How effective are they? Do they help to make the article more picturesque? Tell why.

Good Writers at Work

Examine these figures of speech taken from the works of famous authors. Can you explain why they are effective?

The Commander's voice was like thin ice breaking. —James Thurber

The fog sat like a lid on the mountains and made of the great valley a closed pot. — John Steinbeck

A rusty hinge stood stiffly, like a lonely finger. —Richard Wright

Her breath crowded down under her ribs and grew into a monstrous frightening shape with cutting edges. —Katherine Anne Porter

It seemed to me that people had remodeled their ideas, taken in their convictions a little at the waist, shortened the sleeves of their resolve, and fitted themselves out in a new intellectual design out of the very latest page of history. —E.B. White

For my passion wars against the stiff brocade. —Amy Lowell

Self-reliant like the cat —
that takes its prey to privacy,
the mouse's limp tail hanging like a shoelace from its mouth —
                     — Marianne Moore

The lips of the black-robed judges appeared to me white — whiter than the sheet upon which I trace these words. —Edgar Allan Poe

In the morning, one might say, his face was of a fine florid hue, but after twelve o'clock — his dinner hour — it blazed like a grate full of Christmas coals; and it continued blazing — but, as it were, with a gradual wane — till six o'clock, PM, or thereabouts; after which I saw no more of the proprietor of the face, which, gaining its meridian with the sun, seemed to set with it, to rise, culminate, and decline the following day, with the like regularity and undiminished glory. —Herman Melville

She sat looking about her with eyes as impersonal, almost as stony, as those with which the granite Rameses in a museum watches the froth and fret that ebbs and flows about his pedestal. —Willa Cather

EXPANDING YOUR VOCABULARY

Match the word in Column A with the correct meaning in Column B.

A	B
1. anemia	a. deadly
2. compatible	b. lack of red blood cells
3. condemn	c. annoy; attack
4. contracts (v)	d. transfer of a body organ
5. donor	e. refusing to give up
6. doomed	f. catches
7. fatal	g. to convict
8. persistent	h. one who gives
9. plague (v)	i. agreeing; getting along with
10. transplant (n)	j. facing an unhappy end

Lesson 14
IDIOMS

FEARFUL OF SCHOOL

The first day of each new school year brings with it great excitement, anticipation, goose bumps — and some tears. These feelings are especially in evidence outside the kindergarten classes, where a host of anxious parents, all on tenterhooks, is usually clustered, waiting to see whether their children will have any problems in the new environment.

Each year there are scores of youngsters who are fearful of attending school. They are the square pegs who do not fit into the round holes. At times that fear, or phobia, becomes so severe that the child requires treatment before returning to school. In the New York area, parents can now enroll such youngsters in a school phobia program in the psychiatric clinic at the Long Island Jewish Medical Center.

"Going to school is essentially the child's job," said Dr. Lawrence Sheff, the clinic's director. "We take the bull by the horns by making it clear that this is a non-negotiable item; the child must do his job — he has no choice in the matter. Once that's clear, the parents can see that the child isn't going to fall apart, and the child knows that some other person has taken control of the situation."

How serious can school phobia cases be? Some years ago, a kindergarten child was crying loudly, refusing to follow directions, and disturbing the class on opening day. Her teacher lost patience and decided to take the little girl down a peg by locking her in the clothing closet as punishment. On the floor of the darkened closet were dozens of bean bags which the terrified girl assumed were the bodies of other misbehaving kindergartners. She let out a frightful shriek and fled from the room. It took six years of intensive guidance, pouring oil on troubled waters, to get the child back into fairly regular attendance after that traumatic incident.

Children who are afflicted with school phobia complain about headaches and upset stomachs. They get cold feet at the very mention of school. Toddlers going to school for the first time are not the only ones affected, according to Dr. Sheff. It frequently shows up in older pupils after summer or holiday vacations, or after unsuccessful or humiliating experiences in school.

Dr. Sheff's staff treats the whole family together because they know that a child's anxiety often stems from parental tensions. Then, too, there are cases where a youngster will want to pull up stakes because he is afraid that something will happen to his mother while he is away at school.

The first step in solving the problem, psychiatrists agree, is to make clear to the parents what the phobia is all about. The child is given a direct message that he cannot rule the roost, that he must follow orders and attend school. Next is a period of family therapy to create a better relationship between parents and child as it affects the youngster's fears. In extreme cases, short-term drug therapy is used.

Although there are many painful school phobic cases, the field does have its lighter moments. Psychiatrist Henry Berman is fond of the story about the mother who was urging her fear-ridden son to get out of bed and go to school.

"Mom," he sobbed, "the kids all pick on me, and the teachers hate my guts."

"I know how awful it must be for you, Henry," she pleaded, "but, you must go to school. After all, you are the principal."

TIME TO REMEMBER AND REFLECT

1. According to the article, who can find help at the Long Island Jewish Medical Center?

2. Why did the little kindergarten girl run screaming from the school?

3. When do older children sometimes reveal a school phobia?

4. What are two typical complaints of children who have school phobias?

5. Why do the doctors want to treat the entire family of a child who is fearful about attending school?

6. Did you adjust to kindergarten easily? If so, to what do you attribute that success? If you were one of the difficult cases, how were you helped to overcome your fear?

"RAINING CATS AND DOGS —I STEPPED IN A POODLE"

If you were learning English as a second language, you might be confused by expressions such as "I had to catch a train," "I was sitting on pins and needles," "You can kiss your troubles goodby," and "Don't wash your dirty linen in public." Most newcomers to the language have a devil of a time (oops!) getting at the sense of those expressions, which we call *idioms*, because they are thinking literally rather than figuratively.

Our language is especially rich in idiomatic usage. It is not only important to learn what the idioms mean, but to be able to use them in your own work when they are appropriate. A picturesque idiom can add liveliness and color to your writing.

FAMILIAR IDIOMS

The article in this lesson, "Fearful of School," contains nine familiar idioms:

goose bumps —bumps on the skin, caused by fear
on tenterhooks —in a state of anxiety
square peg in a round hole —out of the ordinary
take the bull by the horns —face a problem directly
take down a peg —deflate, teach a lesson to
pour oil on troubled waters —to calm a situation, restore order
cold feet —hesitation because of fear
pull up stakes —to leave a place, move away
rule the roost —to be in charge

None of these idioms is particularly new. In fact, all could be characterized as cliches. Nevertheless, since it is widespread use that makes an expression into a cliche, you need to know the meanings of those popular expressions, so you can use them when they serve your purpose.

Idioms in Action

When you say, "I caught a cold," "He swallowed his pride," "She spoke tongue in cheek," or "Don't make waves," you are communicating effectively because your audience is generally aware of the meanings of those idioms. At times in the past, however, certain expressions were more relevant than they are today. In fact, people often use idioms without knowing what the phrase originally meant.

To be specific, let's take "on tenterhooks." When you say someone is on tenterhooks, you mean he is very nervous, tense. Tenterhooks are actually small hooks used to stretch fabric tight while it dries. Since very few people weave their own cloth these days, hardly any of the people who use the idiom today have ever seen a tenterhook, let alone know its use. In fact, some think it to be a tender hook. Nowadays, you could find a better way to describe high anxiety.

YOUR TURN

A. Try to discover the origins of the following idioms:

1. to pay the piper
2. the handwriting on the wall
3. a red-letter day
4. a feather in one's cap
5. to pass the buck
6. to know the ropes
7. to strike while the iron is hot
8. to go against the grain
9. to tilt at windmills
10. to raise Cain

B. Turn back to "Fearful of School" and replace each of the eight idioms with your own more pertinent expression. Try to avoid artificial expressions which would not be improvements.

C. Write a composition of about three paragraphs, integrating several of the following idioms:

1. to flog a dead horse
2. to rub a person the wrong way
3. an ax to grind
4. a red herring
5. sour grapes
6. to spill the beans
7. to look a gift horse in the mouth
8. to save face
9. out of the frying pan into the fire
10. to bury the hatchet

EXPANDING YOUR VOCABULARY

Choose the correct meaning for the word in italics.

1. *afflicted* with school phobia   a) made miserable b) treated c) notified
2. director of the *clinic*   a) organization b) project c) institution which provides treatment
3. usually *clustered*   a) scattered b) counted c) gathered
4. *host* of anxious parents   a) membership b) large number c) circle
5. *humiliating* experiences   a) shameful b) thoughtful c) indelible
6. non-*negotiable* items   a) reasonable b) can be settled by bargaining c) appealing
7. *psychiatric* clinic   a) treating emotional disorders b) hospital c) specialized
8. *scores* of youngsters   a) small numbers b) pupils of school age c) large numbers
9. period of family *therapy*   a) decision b) treatment c) compromise
10. *traumatic* incident   a) shocking with lasting effects b) educational c) sentimental

Lesson 15
PAIRED CONSTRUCTIONS

WHAT'S IN A NAME? PLENTY!

Did you hear about the Englishwoman who not only had twins but named them Peter and Repeater? And what do you think of Mr. and Mrs. Fool of Ohio who called their daughter Ima? The Fools might have been loving parents, but you couldn't prove it by their weird judgment in the selection of that name.

Although we say that "sticks and stones may break our bones but names will never harm us," it is obvious that some names can cause terrible embarrassment. If you want proof of that, just ask both Mr. Glittering Diamond of Arkansas and Miss Myrtle Tertel of Pittsburgh. And how about Cant Read of Oklahoma, or Chrystal Shanda Leer of Michigan?

Prof. L.R. Ashley of Brooklyn College, an onomastician (expert on names) and president of the American Name Society, thinks that parents should be very careful when picking names for their children. "Psychological studies," he said, "have demonstrated that names have much to do with how a person learns to cope in the world."

Most of us are familiar with the old joke about the man named Sam Hitler who went to court to have his name changed to…Dave Hitler. But there is nothing funny about the name business to people who are suffering because their parents saddled them with inappropriate names. Our courts receive regular petitions for name changes from men labeled Percy or Throckmorton by thoughtless parents.

Prof. Ashley offers good advice to parents who are getting ready to name their new babies:

Do not pick a dated name (such as Debbie) or an ambiguous one (such as Lee, Robin, or Leslie): the former will give the girl's age away because she was probably named for Debbie Reynolds, while the latter can be used for boys and girls and is therefore confusing.

And be careful about initials. The more that composer Arthur Seymour Sullivan came to think about his initials, the more he hated his parents for them, and we sympathize with him. Finally, since every child has a right to his individuality, he should not be named after his father. Neither John Doe, Jr. nor John Doe III is a wise choice.

The Bureau of the Census reports that the most popular names for American boys and girls traditionally were John and Mary. Today, however, they have been replaced by Michael, Jason, Matthew, Brian, Christopher and David for boys; Jennifer, Amy, Sarah, Michelle, Kimberly, Heather, and Rebecca for girls.

Whatever happened to Gizella Werberzerek Piffle?

TIME TO REMEMBER AND REFLECT

1. What was the unusual name choice of the Fool family of Ohio?

2. Why might Mr. Read of Oklahoma be embarrassed about his name?

3. What was one piece of advice about names given by Prof. Ashley?

4. What is the most popular name given to boys today? To girls?

5. What can people do about names they hate?

6. "What's in a name? That which we call a rose / By any other name would smell as sweet."
   Do you agree with Shakespeare's Juliet that names are not important? Tell why.

7. "We named our first boy John Everett, Jr.," said a lawyer, "and our second son is James Everett III, after my grandfather and father. I don't think that we did the wrong thing, regardless of what Prof. Ashley says." What's your opinion?

BECOMING SENSITIVE TO WRITING STYLES

In every field of endeavor, experience leads to certain sophistication and a degree of expertise. A connoisseur of fine wines is able to appreciate the quality of different grapes and to distinguish among the various products on the market. Art and music lovers, similarly, develop educated tastes about the works of painters and composers. As we learn more about a given subject, we become more sensitive to its fine points, able to see differences we didn't notice at first.

So it is with writing. Many authors have a way of using language, a style, that it is instantly recognizable. If you are a student of literature, you will immediately recognize the author of the following passage from *Youth* as Joseph Conrad:

> A wave of movement passed through the crowd from end to end, passed along the heads, swayed the bodies, ran along the jetty like a ripple on the water, like a breath of wind on a field — and all was still again. I see it now — the wide sweep of the bay, the glittering sands, the wealth of green infinite and varied, the sea blue like the sea of a dream, the crowd of attentive faces, the blaze of vivid colour — the wind reflecting it all, the curve of the shore, the jetty, the high-sterned outlandish craft floating still, and the three boats with the tired men from the West sleeping, unconscious of the land and the people and the violence of sunshine.

The short, punchy sentence structure of Ernest Hemingway is quickly identifiable in this brief sequence from "Fifty Grand":

> "Well," says Jack, "you better go back to town, Soldier."
>
> "What do you mean?"
>
> "You better go back to town and stay there."
>
> "What's the matter?"
>
> "I'm sick of hearing you talk."

"Yes?" says Soldier.

"Yes," says Jack.

"You'll be a damn sight sicker when Walcott gets through with you."

"Sure," says Jack, "maybe I will. But I know I'm sick of you."

So Soldier went off on the train to town that same morning. I went down with him to the train. He was good and sore.

Those with a wide reading background may be able to see the hand of Charles Dickens in this excerpt from *David Copperfield*:

The doctor having been up-stairs and come down again, and having satisfied himself, I suppose, that there was a probability of this unknown lady and himself having to sit there, face to face, for some hours, laid himself out to be polite and social. He was the meekest of his sex, the mildest of little men. He sidled in and out of a room, to take up less space. He walked as softly as the Ghost in *Hamlet*, and more slowly. He carried his head on one side, partly in modest depreciation of himself, partly in modest propitiation of everybody else. It is nothing to say that he hadn't a word to throw at a dog. He couldn't have *thrown* a word at a mad dog. He might have offered him one gently, or half a one, or a fragment of one; for he spoke as slowly as he walked; but he wouldn't have been rude to him, and he couldn't have been quick with him, for any earthly consideration.

PAIRED CONSTRUCTIONS

In summary, therefore, as we become more observant readers, we can detect certain characteristics in writing styles. A careful reader of "What's In a Name? Plenty!" might have noted several sentences that have something in common with respect to their structure and rhythm:

Did you hear about the Englishwoman who *not only* had twins, *but...*

While we say..., it is obvious...

Just as those two...*so has...*

...the former...while the latter...

The more that composer..., *the more* he hated...

Neither John Doe, Jr., *nor* John Doe III...

The italicized words illustrate the technique of using *paired constructions* which appears to be a recurring feature of this particular selection. Many of them use correlative conjunctions, which link words, phrases, or clauses that are similar in their construction. Notice that whenever such a sentence pattern is used, you will find parallel elements — that is, both parts of the construction have the same grammatical structure. For example, in the opening sentence of the reading passage, the conjunctions, *not only...but,* are both followed by verbs, *had* and *named.* The sentence would sound strange and awkward if the author had written: Did you hear about the Englishwoman who not only had twins but their names were Peter and Repeater?
The obvious strength of a paired construction is in its balance and seeming thoughtfulness. When you use a paired construction you are demonstrating that you are capable of planning ahead in a mature fashion, and are not merely putting down words as they pop into your mind.

YOUR TURN

A. Use the following paired constructions in sentences:

either...or
Either we will go to the mountains this summer or we will go to the seashore.

1. not only...but
2. the less...the poorer
3. if not...at least
4. not so...nor as
5. just as...so

B. Write two to three paragraphs on one of the following topics, and use at least six paired constructions in your work:

1. Gun control laws should (should not) be passed by our legislators
2. Coed high schools are better (worse) than single-sex schools
3. I love (hate) talking on the telephone
4. _____ is the cruelest month

WRITING STYLE

This may be an appropriate place to incorporate another important element in your writing — using the right mix of sentence types: simple, compound, complex, loose, periodic and balanced. These are discussed in the last section of your Handbook. As you studied the use of figurative language in Lesson Thirteen, idioms in Lesson Fourteen, and paired constructions in Lesson Fifteen, you began to get an inkling of what constitutes style in writing.

Style is that something extra that lifts your writing from the plain and ordinary — even if it is free of gross errors in grammar and syntax — and makes it distinctive. Style goes a step beyond merely avoiding mistakes. It reflects you —your interests, your knowledge, your personality.

However, while you are growing more sophisticated in employing all the techniques suggested in this book, be careful not to lose the advantages of this improvement by leaving your writing seriously flawed with grammatical errors. That would be like pouring fine wine into a cracked glass.

Study the section in the Handbook that points out how to write effective sentences and shows you how to avoid mistakes that might mar an otherwise excellent story or article.

EXPANDING YOUR VOCABULARY

Match the vocabulary words in Column A with the correct meanings in Column B.

A	B
1. continual	a. burdened
2. cope	b. repeated often
3. demonstrated	c. feeling of being ill at ease
4. embarrassment	d. feel sorry for
5. inappropriate	e. oneness; separate existence
6. individuality	f. easy to understand
7. obvious	g. shown
8. petitions (n)	h. requests
9. saddled	i. get along; manage
10. sympathize	j. not suitable

Lesson 16
THE NEWS STORY

THE USE OF DEADLY FORCE

On the evening of December 8, Manual Marin, a 40-year-old Vineland, New Jersey printer, fired three shots at a man and woman who were ransacking his house. The couple was arrested, but so was Mr. Marin because his state's new penal code makes it a crime to shoot at intruders unless they use or threaten to use deadly force against you.

Thomas W. Cannon of the New Jersey Attorney General's office explained that the new statute was intended "to reduce the use of firearms as much as possible."

One of the arresting officers added, "I know that the new law must seem unjust to Mr. Marin, but without it, we might have every citizen thinking he was John Wayne and firing off shotguns at 14-year-old unarmed burglars."

Mr. Marin is puzzled by the massive attention his case has received. To him, it is an open and shut case. As he reviewed the details of his defense of his home, he could not find that he was guilty of any offense.

"My house had been broken into three times before. When I saw this couple trying to get in, I called the police and got the pistol, for which I have a permit. Meanwhile they started going through the rooms. I came face to face with them in the dining room and ordered them to halt. I fired a warning shot into the ceiling, and when they ran to their car, I got off two shots at their tires."

Mr. Marin's plight has outraged many of his neighbors. Over 3000 people have already signed a petition protesting the law.

"A lot of us are up in arms about this," vehemently declared William Maynard, an elementary school principal. "This law is the final straw. What is society coming to when a man can no longer defend his home without going to jail?"

Raul Rodriguez, a co-worker of Marin's at the Vineland *Journal News*, said, "It's so unfair. Marin has only been in this country ten years, but he's worked hard, bought his own home, and is sending his kids to school. Why is a man like that in trouble because somebody else broke into his home?"

"What's a man supposed to do when he surprises some burglars?" asked neighbor Carmen Abrugiante. "Should he just stand there empty-handed and tell them to stop?"

Another local resident, Helen Bump, gave her opinion: "We're old fashioned Christians, and my husband and I don't like guns. But when something like this happens for the fourth time, a man has a right to do what Mr. Marin did."

Ken Pagliugi, County Prosecutor, announced that Mr. Marin's case will be heard in court this April. "When you have a gun being fired at people, the matter must be decided by a jury of your peers."

The alleged thieves, Aorica Dix, 30, and her brother, Heribito Torres, 18, both Vineland residents, pleaded not guilty at their arraignment. If convicted, they could get a maximum term of five years. It would be ironic if they came face to face with Mr. Marin once again — in jail.

TIME TO REMEMBER AND REFLECT

1. According to the story, why did New Jersey officials pass the new law?

2. What did Mr. Marin's neighbors do to show how they felt about the new law?

3. Why do you think Mr. Marin was allowed to have a gun?

4. Did the two people who were found in Mr. Marin's home admit that they were burglars? What three words in this story could you give in support of your answer?

5. If you read carefully, you should remember the answers: a. How were the thieves related? b. In what city did the story take place? c. How old is Manual Marin?

6. Tell why you agree with the arresting officer ("...we might have every citizen...firing off shotguns at 14-year-old unarmed burglars") or with the elementary school principal ("What is society coming to when a man can no longer defend his home without going to jail?")

7. Every time people organize in order to ban firearms, the representatives of the National Rifle Association remind us, "*Guns* don't kill people; *people* kill people." Explain the meaning of that statement and state your opinion of the controversy.

THE START OF A NEWS STORY

Books on journalism almost always refer to the "5 W's" of a news story: who, what, where, when, why. Those five important questions should be answered within the first paragraph of a news story — preferably within the first sentence. This way, newspaper readers can get the principal facts quickly so they can decide whether to read the rest of that story or to move on to another item in the paper.

who — Manual Marin
what — fired three shots at intruders
where — Vineland, New Jersey
when — evening of December 8
why — they were ransacking his house

OTHER INGREDIENTS OF A GOOD NEWSPAPER STORY

"The Use of Deadly Force" qualifies as an acceptable newspaper story in other ways, too. The reporter had checked out the facts of the case by interviewing the police and a representative of the Attorney General's office. In addition, quotations were provided so that the reader could sense the authenticity of the report.

Furthermore, the reporter offered actual statements from Mr. Marin, three neighbors, a co-worker, and the County Prosecutor. It is apparent to the reader that the journalist used initiative and shoe leather to get the story and to present it in a complete, albeit brief, fashion. Since newspaper space is limited, reporters must get to the point quickly and present supporting material in concise but interesting form.

Balanced Approach

Reporters are expected to be impartial. It is their duty to present the facts of a story and to allow the readers to make up their minds, especially when the incident is controversial. The editorial pages of the paper are reserved for opinions, which are withheld from straight news stories. However, it is not always possible to be absolutely impartial, and reporters have been known to slant their stories in order to reflect their own biases. Reporters with strong feelings about gun control might use their journalistic privilege to present their personal convictions in a favorable light. They can do that, among other ways, by asking belligerent questions of pro-gun people, or by depicting the sorrows of a victim's family in melodramatic fashion. Reporters have been known to interview inarticulate advocates of a certain point of view and then "balance" that with forceful statements from people on the other side of the issue. Their editors are supposed to be alert to such practices, but editors have their biases also.

Stacking the Cards

In "The Use of Deadly Force," the reporter appears to be on Mr. Marin's side in the controversy. We learn that he is a decent, hardworking individual, struggling to put his children through school. He had been victimized on three previous occasions. Solid citizens have spoken out vigorously on his behalf; indeed, 3000 have already signed a petition to free him from prosecution.

As for the other side's point of view, it is presented by means of quotations only from law enforcement officials. Regardless of what they have to say, it is clear that the reader has been manipulated into rooting for Manual Marin to come out on top.

YOUR TURN

A. Turn to "A Mother's Decision," Lesson 18. Rewrite it in the form of a straight news story, remembering to answer the "5 W's" in your opening sentence. Include reports of your interviews with Jerry, Father Tallman, Mrs. D'Aversa, and the police.

B. Turn to "Picking a Valedictorian in Atlantic City," Lesson 23. Rewrite it in the form of a slanted news story in which you try to stack the cards against the teachers who opposed Miss Bahadori's selection as valedictorian.

C. Rewrite "The Use of Deadly Force" to favor the side of the law enforcement officials. You may compose statements from neighbors worried about people who are as "reckless" with firearms as Mr. Marin was.

EXPANDING YOUR VOCABULARY

Choose the correct meaning for the words in italics.

1. not guilty at their *arraignment*   a) arrest   b) indictment   c) pre-trial hearing
2. shoot at *intruders*   a) those who break in   b) spies   c) suspects
3. *massive* attention   a) extensive   b) concerned   c) superficial
4. *maximum* term of five years   a) the least   b) punitive   c) the most
5. jury of your *peers*   a) equals   b) citizens   c) witnesses
6. *penal code*   a) body of law   b) messages   c) endorsements
7. Mr. Marin's *plight*   a) excuses   b) reason for trouble   c) awkward situation
8. were *ransacking* his house   a) looking for things to steal   b) destroying   c) setting fire to
9. new *statute* was intended   a) bronze figure   b) proclamation   c) law
10. he *vehemently* declared   a) subtly   b) with great feeling   c) loudly

Lesson 17
TRANSITIONS

HE HAD A MISSION IN THE WORLD

It was early on a Sunday afternoon at the Staten Island Hospital in New York when 31-year-old Edward Adler went behind the building to his car in the parking lot. Adler, the head of the hospital's blood bank, regularly used his coffee breaks to render the traditional daily prayers that are required of an orthodox Jew. He could not have known it, but he was only a few minutes away from making the most important decision of his young life.

Directly in front of his car, Adler saw a man dragging a nurse into a van at knife point. Without hesitation or regard for his own safety, Adler swiftly rushed to free the struggling woman. Meanwhile, the attacker started the motor in an endeavor to shake Adler off. As the driver slashed at the terrified nurse, the van swerved and sent Adler sprawling to the ground. His head struck the curb, resulting in multiple skull fractures. The nurse was thrown from the van almost immediately, suffering from stab wounds and shock. She would recover, but, the young man who had gallantly saved her would never regain consciousness. A month later, following two operations, good samaritan Edward Adler died as a result of his injuries.

Why had Adler gotten involved? He could have remained in his car, oblivious to the assault. Nevertheless, he responded as his entire life had conditioned him to respond.

His brother, David Adler, said, "What was unusual about Eddie was that he always thought of everyone else first." His father, a high school teacher, agreed: "Furthermore, I am convinced that if Eddie had survived this, he would just as willingly have come to the rescue of some other victim. He had a mission in this world and he fulfilled it."

After the funeral, the grateful nurse wrote to Edward Adler's parents, telling of her sorrow that their son had sacrificed his life to save hers.

"I think I will always feel guilty about that," she said. "I sometimes wish it had been my life instead of his." She ended her letter: "Although he was Jewish and I am Catholic, I will always pray for him."

TIME TO REMEMBER AND REFLECT

1. What did Edward Adler generally do during his afternoon coffee break?

2. What led to Mr. Adler's injuries and ultimate death?

3. Why weren't the other family members surprised that Edward had risked his life to save a stranger?

4. What was Mr. Adler's position at the hospital?

5. What promise did the grateful nurse make to the Adler family?

6. Some people would have done what Edward Adler did. Some would have looked the other way. Is there any way of knowing in advance how a person will react to an emergency?

7. What was Edward's "mission in the world" to which his father referred?

TRANSITIONAL EXPRESSIONS

In a logical style, ideas and actions are strung together in an orderly, meaningful fashion. To provide the logical connections between ideas, successful writers have had to master the use of *transitional expressions*.

You have used transitional expressions without, perhaps, being aware of that label:

1. When you want to show a cause-and-effect relationship, you use *inasmuch as, because, since, as a result of*, and similar words. From the story you just read:

A month later, following two operations, good samaritan Edward Adler died *as a result of* his injuries.

2. When you want to add on another thought, you use words such as *moreover, furthermore, besides*, and *in addition to*:

Furthermore, I am convinced that if Eddie had survived...

3. When you want to indicate chronological order, you use *first, next, prior to, after, meanwhile,* and similar "time" words:

After the funeral...

A month *later,* following two operations...

Meanwhile, the attacker started the motor...

4. When you want to show physical relationships, you use *above, below, behind, in front of, nearby,* and other location words:

...Edward Adler went *behind* the building to his car in the parking lot.

Directly *in front of* his car, Edward saw...

5. When you want to show contrast, you use *although, however, nevertheless, on the other hand, instead,* and similar words:

She would recover; *however,* the young man who had gallantly saved her would never regain consciousness.

Nevertheless, he responded as his entire life had conditioned him to respond.

Although he was Jewish and I am Catholic...

To Do

Read the following passages on the principal as an educational leader. The second treatment has a variety of transitional words in italics. What effect do those words have on the paragraph's composition? Why might some readers describe the second version as "more mature"? Which version do you prefer? Why?

The most important people in the school buildings are the principals. They have the vision that all leaders must possess. The principals set the tone and help to build school morale. The principals serve as the instructional leaders, interpreting the curriculum and helping the teachers to implement it. The principals are the liaisons between the schools and the community. Their expertise and dedication mean a great deal to the schools' progress and achievement. The schools wouldn't close down if the concept of a principal didn't exist; they might have to invent it.

Inasmuch as the most important people in the school building are the principals, they must have the vision that all leaders possess. *Additionally*, the principals set the tone and help to build school morale. *Furthermore*, the principals serve as the instructional leaders, interpreting the curriculum and, *ultimately*, helping the teachers to implement it. The principals, *also*, are the liaisons between the schools and the community. *Finally*, their expertise and dedication mean a great deal to the schools' progress and achievement. *Although* the schools wouldn't close down if the concept of a principal didn't exist, they might have to invent it.

YOUR TURN

A. Write a composition explaining how to do something — build a model, play an electronic game, prepare a meal, etc. Try to use as many transitional expressions of the chronological type as possible.

B. Write a paragraph in which you incorporate the following cause-and-effect words and expressions: since, because, inasmuch as, as a result of.

C. Six soldiers are huddled in a deep trench when a hand grenade is lobbed into their midst. Five scamper away from the deadly device but one soldier throws himself upon the grenade. By taking the full force of the blast, he saves the lives of his otherwise doomed comrades. In a composition (c. 250 words) imagine the kind of man he was, his upbringing, family relationships. Include some possible explanation for his act of heroism.

CONJUNCTIVE ADVERBS

Transitional expressions are frequently conjunctive adverbs. These are more fully discussed in the adverb section of the Handbook (page 132).

EXPANDING YOUR VOCABULARY

Choose the correct meaning of the italicized words in the sentences. Use the context as a clue.

1. oblivious   a) caught off guard   b) unprepared   c) not aware   d) involved
2. assault   a) intention   b) attack   c) insult   d) confusion

Inasmuch as he was praying, he could have remained in his car, *oblivious* to the *assault*.

3. endeavor   a) motion   b) maneuver   c) trick   d) attempt

Meanwhile, the attacker started the motor car in an *endeavor* to shake Adler off the bumper of the van.

4. multiple   a) more than one   b) serious   c) fatal   d) compound

His head struck the curb, resulting in *multiple* skull fractures.

5. render   a) select   b) sing   c) compose   d) perform
6. traditional   a) customary   b) prescribed   c) holy   d) lengthy
7. orthodox   a) believing   b) rabbinical   c) strictly religious   d) educated

Mr. Adler, the head of the hospital blood bank, regularly used his coffee breaks to *render* the *traditional* daily prayers which are required of an *orthodox* Jew.

8. samaritan   a) medical student   b) businessman   c) one who acts hastily   d) one who helps unselfishly

A month later, following two operations, good *samaritan* Edward Adler died as a result of his injuries.

9. served   a) raced off   b) stalled   c) turned   d) sputtered
10. sprawling   a) crashing   b) tumbling   c) bouncing   d) injured

As the driver slashed at the terrified nurse, his vehicle *swerved* and sent Edward *sprawling* to the ground.

Lesson 18
POINT OF VIEW

A MOTHER'S DECISION

When Rita D'Aversa got home from shopping at the A&P, she noticed that her son had closed his bedroom door, something that 16-year-old Jerry never did. Tiptoeing up the steps, Mrs. D'Aversa heard voices in Jerry's room, and she opened the door swiftly without knocking. Seated on the bed, counting a huge stack of dollar bills, were Jerry and his best friend Dom.

"What's this?" Mrs. D'Aversa asked.

"We found some money," Jerry stammered.

But when Mrs. D'Aversa questioned the boys closely, she had reason to doubt their veracity. Apparently they were lying, and she was determined to get at the truth.

There was an envelope protruding from Jerry's zipper jacket, which hung behind the door. Before Jerry could snatch it out of her hands, Rita recognized it as a collection envelope from the neighboring St. Barnabas church.

"This is church money," Mrs. D'Aversa shouted. "You ought to be ashamed of yourself for thinking of keeping it. You and Dom just get your coats on and take it right back to St. Barnabas. Every penny!"

After the two boys had left, looking sulky and resentful, to return the $217 bonanza, Mrs. D'Aversa continued to fret about the matter. Finally, she telephoned St. Barnabas and asked to speak to Father Tallman, the pastor. Although he was busy with detectives at the time, Father Tallman came to the phone.

"Did the church lose some money, Father?" Mrs. D'Aversa asked nervously. "It's important."

"We did indeed," came the reply. "Two teenage boys held up Father O'Shea after mass and stole the entire collection. Do you know something about it, Madam?" As the priest spoke, he was signalling to a detective to pick up the extension phone.

Mrs. D'Aversa gasped at the news of the robbery and hung up quickly. Jerry had been involved in some silly pranks but never anything so insane as robbery. And at a church, no less!

A widow for the past twelve years, Rita D'Aversa had done her best to raise her daughter and Jerry as God-fearing, religious children. She was staggered by the enormity of the crime and what it signified. The least of it would be the return of the money. If she informed the police, her son would be arrested and his entire future placed in jeopardy. If she didn't, would he ever understand how wrong what he did was?

She sat down to cry, her body wracked with sobs of anguish. After a few terrible minutes, she dialed the telephone operator.

"Give me the police," Mrs. D'Aversa said.

TIME TO REMEMBER AND REFLECT

1. Why did Mrs. D'Aversa tiptoe up the stairs to her son's bedroom?

2. Why did Mrs. D'Aversa feel that she had to telephone the St. Barnabas church?

3. Why did Mrs. D'Aversa hang up when the priest asked her what she knew about the theft?

4. Are you good at recalling details? What was Jerry's friend's name? Was Jerry an only child? What was the name of the pastor? What was the name of the priest who had been held up?

5. What evidence was there in the story to lead you to feel that Mrs. D'Aversa would turn her son in to the police?

6. Should Mrs. D'Aversa have notified the police about her son's crime? What would you have done if you were in her place? Did her decision indicate that she cared for her son or did not care for him? Tell why.

7. Is stealing money from a religious institution a worse offense than stealing it from a private business? Why? What punishment would you give to 16-year-old Jerry if you were judging his case?

POINT OF VIEW

The opening story in this book, "Now You See It..." is told in the first person, from the point of view of one of the characters. The "I" of that story is the schoolboy who found the gun in his desk and was advised to forget about it. One advantage in presenting a work of fiction in that way is that the narrator can express his feelings directly to the reader. In addition, he is an active figure in the events that are unfolding. It tends to personalize the story and to heighten the suspense.

"A Mother's Decision," however, is told from the conventional third-person point of view. The story, in effect, is related by someone outside, who knows everything that is taking place without actually taking part in the story. As readers, we learn what is going on in the minds of all the characters; we are denied nothing.

Making Use of Point of View

Both techniques have been used successfully, but the all-knowing third person is more common. Writers feel that they are in greater control with it, being able to focus on details, guide the readers, and draw conclusions. With the first-person technique writers have to be careful to limit themselves to the viewpoint of a single character, and not let out any information that character couldn't have.

If "A Mother's Decision" had been only Rita D'Aversa's story, told by her, certain details would have had to be omitted. For example, we could not have known that detectives were already investigating the church robbery, or that one of them had been told to pick up the extension phone. While such items may not be critical to this particular story, it is easy to see that their importance could be significant in some other piece of writing.

In Summary

Before starting to write a story, you should decide on the best point of view to employ. If you want to tell the story the way it appeared to a single character, use the "I" method. If you think that your canvas will be enriched by an all-knowing third person, by all means tell it that way. Be aware of the different options open to you and their inherent values.

Some writers are comfortable with first-person narratives, some with third-person, and others with flexible organizations which allow them to be involved in the action at times, but outside the action as observers at other times. Kurt Vonnegut used this technique in his novel *Slaughterhouse Five*. Robert Penn Warren's celebrated novel, *All the King's Men* is another example of how a master craftsman can make use of this approach to point of view.

When you read other stories, ask yourself these questions about point of view:

1. What person is the story written in — first or third — and why?
2. Is the narrator all-knowing (omniscient)? Is the narrator an outsider or involved in the plot?
3. How reliable is the narrator? Should we question the narrator's perception?
4. Does the point of view change?
5. Would the work be different if told from a different point of view?

YOUR TURN

A. Rewrite "A Mother's Decision" in the first person with Mrs. D'Aversa as the participant. Your first sentence: "When I got home from shopping at the A&P, I was surprised to see that my son Jerry's bedroom door was shut."

B. Turn back to the first story, "Now You See It..." and rewrite it from the third-person point of view. Your opening sentence: "On his first day at Filmore High School, Larry Foster found more excitement than he had bargained for."

C. Turn to the story which precedes this one, "He Had a Mission in the World," and rewrite it from the point of view of the nurse who had been saved. What difficulties do you anticipate before you start?

D. Compare any one of your versions with the original story. In what way is yours better? In what way is the original better? What have you learned in the process of taking the story apart and putting it back together in a different form?

EXPANDING YOUR VOCABULARY

Match the words in Column A with the meanings in Column B.

A	B
1. anguish (n)	a. to worry
2. bonanza	b. pieces of mischief
3. enormity	c. great suffering
4. fret	d. tormented
5. ostensibly	e. source of great profit
6. pranks	f. truthfulness
7. protruding	g. meant
8. signified	h. extreme wickedness
9. veracity	i. sticking out
10. wracked	j. according to appearances

Lesson 19
EDITORIAL ESSAYS

WE MIGHT AS WELL LIVE

On one hand we are told by statisticians that we are living longer than our ancestors did. On the other hand, however, each new day brings chilling warnings of imminent doom from scientists, nutritionists, and environmentalists. It's hard to know whether the 1980s are a time to rejoice about our good fortune or to weep bitter tears about the horrible mess we are in.

Do you like peanut butter? A testing laboratory has said watch out. Are you fond of that great American breakfast of ham 'n eggs and coffee? All can kill us, we are warned. Are no-calorie cola drinks on your menu because you are trying to lose weight? Haven't you heard what those beverages do to laboratory mice!

The list goes on and on. Dandruff lotion is a no-no; drinking water in most localities is suspect; pills for insomnia might induce cancer. There's mercury in the innocent swordfish, which won't do our brains one bit of good, and the beef we eat carries vile chemicals into our unsuspecting tummies. Even a seemingly wholesome liquid such as mother's milk has been labeled a possible source of trouble. It appears that nothing is sacred.

If foods and beverages won't get us, we can expect to be finished off by the poisoned atmosphere and acid rain. And a cool swim in the polluted old mill stream is almost akin to suicide, some environmentalists would have us believe.

What to do about it all is the big problem. We can't even brood about our melancholy condition because it has just been reported that worrying about cancer can cause cancer. In a society where t-shirts carry the message "Life is hazardous to your health," we have to fight against the kind of pessimism that can paralyze us. It may be wise to pay attention to the experts, but at the same time we must trust that man will survive in spite of the quicksand threatening to swallow him up.

TIME TO REMEMBER AND REFLECT

1. What good fortune could a modern person rejoice about, according to the article?

2. Name two foods which were said to be hazardous to our health.

3. Why are we told not to worry about so serious a disease as cancer?

4. What was the humorous message which appeared on a t-shirt?

5. What advice did the author give at the end of the article?

6. An accountant was heard to say, "I could follow the advice of health nuts and eat a restricted diet, but I'd rather enjoy my life with steaks and apple pie." What is your opinion of that philosophy?

7. What is the meaning of the last sentence of the article? If you accept its message, how will that affect your own way of life?

THINK PIECE

"We Might As Well Live" is written in the manner of the editorials which appear in many daily newspapers. It deals with a serious subject, presents a good deal of information, and concludes with the writer's (newspaper's) policy decision.

To be specific, we are surveying some of the dangers of life in the closing decades of the 20th century. The writer tells us about the foods which can make us sick, as well as the environmental hazards that are hastening us into the grave. All of this is dreadfully pessimistic — until the editorial's punch line: We should remember that man has continued to survive in the face of all obstacles and terrors, and it is reasonable to assume that he will overcome these formidable threats as well.

Up for Grabs

Certain editorial writers serve up controversial subjects without ever taking a clear position on either side of the problem. When the matter is a particularly hot potato, they are loath to alienate a whole group of readers who already have taken sides on the issue. (See "Pinned to the Mat," page 28, and "The Klansman and the Diploma," page 39, for editorial-type articles that present both sides of a dilemma and actually invite the reader to make up his own mind.)

Using Irony to Make a Point

On occasion, an editorialist will imply that something is wrong, often relying upon irony to make his point. The melancholy descriptions of the senior citizens who are "killing time" in the gambling casinos ("Having Fun in Our Town," page 10) are a good example of this technique. For a further discussion of the use of irony in writing, see "Opening a Can of Worms," page 98.

YOUR TURN

A. Write an editorial in the manner of "We Might As Well Live" that introduces a subject, offers additional information on it, and then concludes with an opinion. You may select one of the following topics:

1. Sending Food to Needy People in Communist Countries
2. Taxing Childless Families to Support Schools
3. Drafting Women Into the Armed Forces

B. Write an editorial which presents both sides of a controversial matter but stops short of taking a position. You may select one of the following topics:

1. Fighting on the Hockey Ice
2. Using Life Support Systems to Keep the Terminally Ill Alive
3. Allowing Corporal Punishment in Our Schools

EXPANDING YOUR VOCABULARY

Choose the correct meaning of the italicized words in the sentences. Use the context as a clue.

1. polluted   a) chemically treated   b) made impure   c) rain-swollen   d) blocked with logs
2. akin   a) painful   b) cruel   c) certain   d) similar

A cool swim in a *polluted* old mill stream is almost *akin* to suicide.

3. imminent   a) important   b) slow   c) about to happen   d) predictable
4. nutritionist   a) calorie counter   b) vitamin expert   c) health addict   d) food specialist
5. environmentalist   a) one who frowns on smoking   b) one who is concerned about our surroundings   c) an animal lover   d) a biologist

On the other hand, however, each new day brings chilling warnings of *imminent* doom from scientists, *nutritionists*, and *environmentalists*.

6. insomnia   a) poor digestion   b) inability to sleep   c) mental disorder   d) overweight
7. induce   a) to develop   b) to prevent   c) to cause   d) to screen

Pills for *insomnia* might *induce* cancer.

8. persevere   a) survive   b) take life as it comes   c) stumble along in ignorance   d) keep doing something in spite of difficulties

We must acknowledge that man will *persevere* in spite of the quicksand which is threatening to swallow him up.

9. statistician   a) medical expert   b) mathematician   c) insurance agent   d) expert on statistics

On one hand we are told by *statisticians* that we are living longer than our parents did.

10. vile   a) poisonous   b) explosive   c) foul   d) enriched
The beef we eat could transmit *vile* chemicals into our unsuspecting tummies.

Lesson 20
MATTERS OF FACT

MR. BANFI'S LOTION

Poor people often dream about ways to make huge sums of money. If they could only invent a product that everyone needs — stockings that never tear, tires that cannot wear out or blow out, a substitute for gasoline — or find a way to eliminate cancer or heart disease, they could be rolling in wealth.

Andras Banfi, a Hungarian factory worker, claims to have discovered something that could make him a millionaire many times over —a cure for baldness!

While studying ancient Egyptian manuscripts, Mr. Banfi said he came across a formula that supposedly would grow hair on the shiniest of bald domes. When he marketed it (*Mr. Banfi's Lotion*) in Budapest, long lines formed in front of the shops that featured his product. Police had to be called out to maintain order as the eager customers surged forward to snatch at the remaining bottles on the counters.

Even though there is no proof that the mixture works, Hungarians are happily smearing it on their heads, and Mr. Banfi has become as wealthy as any Arab oil man. In fact, smugglers have been asking up to $100 per bottle in Vienna, Athens, and Prague.

Since the Hungarian's product has a horrible, garlic-like smell, and there is absolutely no scientific proof of its effectiveness, it is amazing that people are so eager to buy it. Obviously, a luxuriant head of hair is so important to bald-headed men that they are willing to take a chance on a longshot such as Banfi's hair restorer.

One thing which should discourage the customers is that Mr. Banfi never allows his picture to be taken unless he is wearing his hat. We wonder why.

TIME TO REMEMBER AND REFLECT

1. According to the article, what is one way to become rich, aside from finding a cure for baldness?

2. Where did Mr. Banfi get the idea for his sensational product?

3. Why have smugglers become involved with *Mr. Banfi's Lotion*?

4. What evidence is there in the article to show that people are willing to sacrifice in order to grow hair on their heads?

5. How can you tell whether or not the author of the article believes in the effectiveness of the hair oil?

6. People who are bald feel that they will look younger if they had hair on their heads. Why do people think it important to look young?

7. Studies have shown that no matter how far-fetched your claim is for a health product (eliminate wrinkles, make ugly fat disappear, provide new vigor), customers will want it. Why are people so willing to let themselves by misled by such obviously false claims?

FACT AND OPINION

A fact is verifiable. An opinion is a judgment or a belief. *Hank Aaron is the all-time home run king of baseball.* This fact can be checked in the record books. *The ability to debate is an essential skill for presidential candidates.* That is an opinion, which may or may not be upheld in the future. Simple honesty demands that you not confuse facts and opinions. You should not invent facts to suit your purposes, slant an apparently objective story by omitting or over-emphasizing one side, or change data in any way. This is particularly true in expository writing and argumentation, where a conclusion will be based on the facts presented.

A statement beginning "Everyone knows that..." or "It is generally accepted that..." may be true, or it may be hiding an opinion disguised as a fact. It is your job to check the validity of such statements by asking: Where is this fact stated? How can it be verified? Is the writer qualified through experience, expertise, education, or personal observation to make this statement? Does the statement contradict other authorities or your own observations? Only after such probing analysis can you accept the fact as presented.

A Genuine Cure?

Note the care taken in the article "*Mr. Banfi's Lotion*" not to give the impression that Mr. Banfi's cure actually works.

...he *claims* to have found a cure for baldness.

...came across a formula which *supposedly* would grow hair

Even though there is *no proof* that the mixture works...

...and there is *absolutely no scientific proof of its effectiveness*

...they are willing *to take a chance on a longshot.*

Even the last sentence is a tongue-in-cheek admission that something may be rotten in Budapest.

Just the Facts, Ma'am

Now, let's examine the article again, this time selecting statements presented as facts.

- Andras Banfi, a Hungarian factory worker, discovered something that would make him a millionaire many times over.
- Police had to be called out to maintain order.
- Smugglers are asking up to $100 per bottle.
- The product has a horrible garlic-like smell.
- Mr. Banfi never allows his picture to be taken unless he is wearing his hat. Are these verifiable? How?

MISLEADING THE READER

Just as you should not manipulate facts to arrive at an unjustified conclusion, you should also avoid deceptive language. There are many ways to write deceptively, including slanting, labeling, and shifting meanings.

Slanting

"How do you know?" sneered Mrs. Smith.
"I have made a careful study of the matter," Mrs. Jones replied courteously.

Even without knowing what they are talking about, we tend to assume that Mrs. Smith is the one in the wrong, because nice people don't sneer, and that the courteous Mrs. Jones is right. However, consider the same passage with a couple of changes:

"How do you know?" asked Mrs. Smith curiously.

"I have made a careful study of the matter," Mrs. Jones replied smugly.

Now it sounds as if the curious Mrs. Smith is right, since we automatically want someone smug to be wrong. But we still don't know what they are talking about. We are being influenced by slanted language.

Labeling

How can you even think of voting for an unsavory character like Mr. Nolte?

Has anything been proved against Mr. Nolte? If not, you are just labeling him by calling him unsavory; that is, by your words you are implying something that, in justice, ought to be proved. By using either complimentary or derogatory words — honest, boneheaded, egghead, first-rate, inferior, racist —you are replacing reason with prejudice and emotion.

Shifting Meanings

Writers are guilty of shifting the meanings of words when they take abstract terms that have a wide range of meaning and use those terms to mean different things. Consider the following passage:

People complain about the lack of freedom in countries that don't have democratic elections, but look at the way some teenagers talk back to their teachers and disobey their parents. I say you can have too much freedom!

In the first sentence, freedom means the political right to vote, but in the last sentence it means the absence of restraint. By shifting the meaning of the word, the author makes it look as if the two situations described here are connected, even though there is actually no logical connection.

Language is a powerful tool. As a reader, you must be on guard to make sure no one is trying to trick you. As a writer, you have a responsibility to use language honestly.

YOUR TURN

A.   Which of the following are facts and which are opinions?

1.   Thomas Jefferson was the third President of the United States.
2.   The Caspian Sea is larger than Lake Superior.
3.   The Verrazano Narrows Bridge is the most beautiful suspension bridge in the world.
4.   Alaska is the largest state of the union.

5. Ice hockey is the world's most exciting sport.
6. The flags of Israel and Guatemala use the same colors.
7. Dave Winfield was the most outstanding player on the New York Yankees.
8. The metric system is easier to deal with than our present system of weights and measures.
9. The Russian invasion of Afghanistan was unjustified.
10. Gas heats best.

B. Comment on the logic or illogic of each of the following statements:

1. I call on you to reject this wasteful, unnecessary expenditure which can only multiply our problems.
2. This great and good man, whose dedication to freedom and justice is known to all of us, deserves your support.
3. The youth of today are not at all like those of the past generation.
4. Mr. Blanding is, after all, a politician, with all the vices that normally go with this profession.
5. His claim to be a world traveler is well-founded. I have seen his collection of artifacts from many different countries.

C. Choose one side of a controversial issue and write a well-organized paragraph, citing at least five facts that lead you to your opinion. If you do not have a topic you feel strongly about, consider one of the following:

1. Should the President be elected by popular vote?
2. Should TV be censored?
3. Should we permit animal vivisection?
4. Should we reinstate the draft?
5. Should prayers be permitted in the public schools?

EXPANDING YOUR VOCABULARY

Match the word in Column A with the meaning in Column B.

A	B
1. ancient	a. one who exports or imports illegally
2. discourage	b. sold
3. eliminate	c. get rid of
4. featured	d. old
5. formula	e. a way of doing something
6. luxuriant	f. moved suddenly
7. manuscript	g. to make less hopeful
8. marketed	h. abundant
9. smuggler	i. written document
10. surged	j. advertised

Lesson 21
CREATING ATMOSPHERE WITH CONNOTATIONS

THE GUARDIAN ANGELS

New Yorker Arnold Johnson was about to be robbed. It was 2 a.m. when Johnson saw the teenager swagger through the subway train door at the 149th Street IRT station in the Bronx, and he knew that young man spelled trouble.

"Let's have the money, Pops, and be quick about it." The speaker, who had his leather jacket open to show Johnson the gun stuck in his belt, slapped the old man viciously, knocking out his false teeth. Just as the frightened Johnson fished for his wallet, the car door opened and four fellows with red berets rushed in to seize the assailant. At the next stop they turned him over to a Transit Authority policeman, returned Johnson's dentures to him, and saw that he got home safely.

For more than six months the Magnificent 13 (the group's first name) had been patrolling New York City's most dangerous subway routes in order to thwart the muggers. The original group was founded by Curtis Sliwa, a 26-year-old former manager of a McDonald's restaurant, because he felt that the police were fighting a losing battle against the "bad guys."

Sliwa's group was a United Nations mixture of public-spirited youths: whites, blacks, Hispanics, and Chinese. Every evening at 9 p.m. Sliwa divided his troops into small squads and sent them off, unarmed, to help maintain law and order in the city's perilous subway atmosphere.

"You've got to have a job or be going to school to become a member," said Sliwa. He trained them in crime prevention techniques, showing the recruits how to spot a pickpocket and how to disarm a mugger.

The police haven't been too cooperative because they distrust vigilantes, but as one sergeant put it: "Let's face it, we're happy for whatever help we can get. If I'm going to war in the subway every night, I like to have as many loyal soldiers on my side as I can get."

Curtis Sliwa's original group has grown steadily until it now numbers close to a thousand. They have gone beyond their original subway mission, now offering aid to people who are so afraid that they rarely leave home.

It's hard to predict how long the Guardian Angels, as they have come to be known, will continue to render their unique service, but they are encouraged by the Arnold Johnsons of the city who say, "The boys make me feel safe again."

TIME TO REMEMBER AND REFLECT

1. Why did Mr. Johnson's attacker keep his jacket open?

2. Why did Curtis Sliwa decide to form the Magnificent 13?

3. What is one requirement for membership in the Guardian Angels?

4. What indication is there that the group of volunteers has been successful so far?

5. Why do the police have mixed feelings about the young vigilantes?

6. A fireman said, "When I was in junior high, they tried to pick all the tough guys and put them on hall patrol. It didn't work out then and it won't work out now." Tell whether you agree or disagree with that statement, as it affects the Guardian Angels.

7. Curtis Sliwa meets regularly with elected officials and has gained reluctant recognition from them. His marriage to a Guardian Angel leader in 1981 attracted several thousand well-wishers and reporters from all the television stations. His Guardian Angels have come a long way since their first subway patrols. Would you want the young vigilantes to help with a criminal problem in your town? Why?

CREATING ATMOSPHERE

You are at home in the evening and you turn on the TV. What program will you watch? Sometimes you select a serious dramatic program, other times a musical revue, still other times a ball game or a talk show. Why the changes? Generally, you choose a program which fits your mood. You would not remain with a program that "switched gears" without reason or that failed to deliver what you had expected.

When you are the writer, you must also make certain that your tone and your words all build up and contribute to the kind of mood and atmosphere you have decided upon. Note how "The Guardian Angels" begins by setting the stage for the assault on the innocent subway rider: "New Yorker Arnold Johnson was about to be robbed." The situation is described and the action moves quickly from the attempted mugging to the happy ending.

Choosing Your Words Carefully

More than that. Specific words were intentionally chosen that not only tell you what happened but also convey a definite feeling. Words were chosen not just for their literal meanings, but also for their connotations, what they imply or suggest. The teenager did not *walk* through the subway door. He *swaggered*. He did not merely act *suspiciously*. He *spelled trouble*. The connotations of these words and phrases make the reader distrust the teenager.

Look further. The gun-toting teenager "slapped the old man viciously and knocked out his false teeth." Would your revulsion be as strong if the writer had said, "The armed robber struck Mr. Johnson hard"? And did you follow the heroes, who didn't merely run to Mr. Johnson's aid but "rushed in to seize the assailant." Furthermore, how gratified you are when the writer points up the quiet efficiency of the Guardian Angels who, without fanfare, accomplish three objectives — they turn over the assailant to the authorities, courteously return Mr. Johnson's dentures, and cap their heroism by seeing him home safely. Every word and action was clearly intended to make you regard the rescuers with kindliness, sympathy and appreciation. What you have seen illustrated is the deliberate choice of words and incidents to create an atmosphere, a mood, or an attitude.

To summarize, connotative words suggest clear images, pictures, and moods you seek to express. Connotations, properly used, will help your readers to see and feel what you intend.

YOUR TURN

A. Analyze the fourth and the last paragraph of the selection for connotations that create moods and attitudes. Discuss the merit of expressions such as "public spirited," "to help maintain law and order," and "unique services" in this context.

B. Explain the difference between:

1. *hopeless* and *desperate*
2. *heavy* and *massive*
3. *small* and *infinitesimal*
4. *take* and *snatch*
5. *pull* and *haul*

Describe a situation in which the second word in each pair is more appropriate than the first.

C. Expand each expression into a description that conveys a strong mood or definite picture:

1. a cranky child
2. a lazy student
3. a brilliant play
4. an exciting game
5. a delicious dessert
6. a beautiful dress
7. a humorous cartoon
8. a busy street
9. a mean person
10. a catchy advertisement

D. For one of the following topics write a narrative of 200 words. Try to create and sustain a definite mood by the liberal use of words rich in connotations.

1. Lost at Sea
2. First Flight
3. Once Was Too Much
4. The Tables Are Turned
5. Rescued

EXPANDING YOUR VOCABULARY

Choose the correct meaning of the italicized words in the sentences. Use the context as a clue.

1. assailant   a) drunkard   b) criminal   c) attacker   d) patriot

Four fellows with red berets rushed in to seize the *assailant*.

2. dentures   a) wallet   b) false teeth   c) spectacles   d) papers

At the next step they turned him over to a Transit Authority policeman, returned Johnson's *dentures* to him, and saw that he got home safely.

3. maintain   a) uphold   b) arrest   c) undergo   d) justify

4. perilous   a) dangerous   b) unusual   c) lively   d) crowded

Every evening at 9 p.m. Sliwa divided his troops into small squads and sent them off, unarmed, to help *maintain* law and order in the city's *perilous* subway atmosphere.

5. recruit   a) youngsters   b) volunteers   c) players   d) new members

He trains them in crime prevention techniques, showing the *recruits* how to spot a pickpocket and how to disarm a mugger.

6. swagger   a) rush   b) strut   c) meander   d) crash

It was 2 a.m. when Johnson saw the teenager *swagger* through the subway train door.

7. thwart   a) identify   b) capture   c) keep from success   d) handcuff

For more than six months, the Magnificent 13 had been patrolling New York City's most dangerous subway routes in order to *thwart* the muggers.

8. unique   a) timely   b) one of a kind   c) regular   d) necessary

It's hard to predict how long the Guardian Angels will continue to render their *unique* service.

9. viciously   a) lightly   b) accidentally   c) deliberately   d) cruelly

The speaker slapped the old man *viciously*.

10. vigilantes   a) groups of teenagers   b) those who take the law into their own hands
c) musicians   d) suspects

The police haven't been too cooperative because they distrust *vigilantes*.

Lesson 22
VARYING SENTENCES

THE NATIVES WERE FRIENDLY

(1) In addition to July 4, there are some other well-known days on our calendar: February 12 (Lincoln's Birthday), February 22 (Washington's Birthday), June 6 (D-Day), December 7 (Pearl Harbor), etc. (2) But does December 2 mean anything special to you?

(3) It really should because on the bleak afternoon of that day in 1942 a memorable drama took place on an abandoned squash court under the stands of Stagg Field, the University of Chicago's stadium.

(4) The curtain on that drama actually rose in Rome, Italy on September 29, 1901 when Enrico Fermi was born. (5) As soon as the little boy could talk it became obvious that he was a prodigy — an exceptionally brilliant child. (6) Fermi swept through the best Italian schools with ease and became such an outstanding physicist that he was awarded the Nobel Prize in 1938.

(7) Shortly after coming to live in the United States, he got President Roosevelt's approval to do secret work in the field of atomic energy research. (8) We were in an all-out race to produce an atomic bomb before the Germans did, and Fermi's work was given the highest priority. (9) On December 2, 1942 the big moment had arrived. (10) A huge pile of graphite layers and uranium chunks confronted the invited scientists and military observers when they entered the old squash court in Chicago. (11) The uranium gave off neutrons at a steady rate while the graphite slowed down the speed of neutrons. (12) Cadmium rods had been inserted in holes in the pile because they absorbed neutrons effectively. (13) Three brave young men were crouched atop the pile, ready to drench it with liquid cadmium should something go wrong. (14) As the cadmium rods were slowly removed, the chain reaction Fermi was striving for took place.

(15) All of the measuring devices told the scientists that Fermi's work was a success. (16) An atomic bomb could be built and controlled. (17) The United States had achieved the supreme offensive and defensive weapon before our enemies could attain it.

(18) Prof. Fermi placed a coded telephone call to his superior at Harvard University.

(19) "The Italian Navigator has reached the New World," he said.

(20) "And how did he find the natives?" came the question.

(21) "Very friendly," Fermi replied.

(22) On December 2, 1992 the 50th anniversary of that landmark day will be celebrated.

TIME TO REMEMBER AND REFLECT

1. Which four well-known days on our calendar are referred to in the article?

2. Where did the famous chain reaction trial take place?

3. Why were the three young assistants stationed on top of the pile of graphite and uranium?

4. What code name was used to identify Enrico Fermi? Why was it necessary to use a code name?

5. What was the meaning of Fermi's message, "The natives were friendly."?

6. What might a Japanese scientist whose family was killed at Hiroshima say about the achievement of Enrico Fermi?

7. One of Fermi's friends had said that he would help Enrico in any way but would never work on a bomb which might be used to kill people. What is your opinion of that scientist's position?

VARYING SENTENCE BEGINNINGS

An entire section of the chapter entitled "Writing Effective Sentences" (page 171) is devoted to variations in normal word order. Let's look at the structure of "The Natives Were Friendly" to see this technique in action.

Normally the sentence parts are placed in this order: subject, verb, completers. Occasionally, it is advisable to shift to a transposed or inverted word order, placing the verb before the subject, or to gain variety by placing a modifying word, phrase, or dependent clause before the subject of the main clause.

The sentences in the reading selection have been numbered for easy identification:
Sentence 1 begins with a prepositional phrase and inverts the subject and predicate.
Sentence 2 asks a question.
Sentences 5 and 14 begin with an adverbial clause.
Sentence 7 begins with an adverb modifying a prepositional phrase.
Sentences 9 and 22 begin with prepositional phrases.
Sentences 19 to 21 are direct quotations.

THE LONG AND SHORT OF IT

A second device has been employed to achieve variety and suspense in this narrative: short, dramatic sentences combined with the longer sentences of explanation. See sentences 9 and 16 and the cryptic telephone conversation of sentences 19 to 21. In addition, the narrative uses the passive voice in sentences 4, 6, 8, 12, 14, 16, and 22 without slowing the dramatic action or distracting us from the main point — Fermi's steady progress toward the successful building of an atomic bomb. Note that in several of these sentences the passive voice is used in the dependent clause ("when Enrico Fermi *was born*," "he *was awarded* the Nobel Prize," "as the rods *were removed*"). In the other sentences the active voice would have been awkward ("Cadmium rods *had been inserted*," because it is not important to tell who actually inserted the rods). The last sentence properly stresses the 50th anniversary by making it the subject of the passive verb instead of using the more awkward construction: "We will celebrate the 50th anniversary of that landmark day."

One point bears repetition: only occasionally should the normal word order be changed. Too much variety will make your writing seem stilted and unnatural. Equally important is the need to vary the sentence length and type: short and long; simple, compound, and complex; declarative, interrogative, imperative, and exclamatory; and direct quotation and narrative. Such combinations and variations are pleasing, balanced, and effective.

YOUR TURN

A. Identify the change from the normal word order in the following sentences:

1. While studying ancient Egyptian manuscripts, Mr. Banfi came across a formula which supposedly would grow hair on the shiniest of bald domes.
2. Even though there is no proof that the mixture works, Hungarians are happily smearing it on their heads.
3. Now a blind woman can get a job as a sportswriter.
4. Convinced that her male colleagues have an unfair advantage over her, she decided to go to court.
5. In a recent movie, actor Charles Bronson's wife was killed by some neighborhood hoodlums.
6. To pass the tests, some students had to resort to cheating.
7. Everything he can resist except temptation.
8. The last bus loaded with children having departed, we heaved a sigh of relief.

B. Collect at least ten sentences using different patterns of word order. Be prepared to discuss their effectiveness.

C. Write a narrative of 200 words using some of the sentence patterns discussed in this chapter: transposed word order, subject preceded by word, phrase, or clause modifiers, sentences varying in type and length, active and passive verbs. Suggested topics:

1. It Was Unavoidable
2. What Are Friends for?
3. It Was Fun, but —
4. The Secret Guest
5. An Innocent Remark

EXPANDING YOUR VOCABULARY

Match the words in Column A with the meanings in Column B.

A	B
1. absorbed	a. tiny particle in an atom
2. attain	b. for self-protection
3. bleak	c. to reach
4. defensive	d. important event
5. landmark	e. chilly; raw
6. neutron	f. for attack
7. offensive	g. high level of importance
8. priority	h. very talented person
9. prodigy	i. trying
10. striving	j. soaked

Lesson 23
APPOSITIVES, PREDICATE NOMINATIVES, AND RELATIVE CLAUSES

PICKING A VALEDICTORIAN IN ATLANTIC CITY

In the spring of 1980, United States feelings toward Iran were inflamed because 53 Americans were still being held hostage by Moslem militants. Since ours is a shrinking world, that unlawful action taken halfway around the globe had its effect on a graduation in New Jersey.

The top seniors at Atlantic City High School had been invited to compete for the honor of delivering the valedictory address at their commencement exercises. The winner, a straight A student, was Tina Bahadori, an 18-year-old who had come to this country a year and a half earlier. Miss Bahadori, an Iranian national, was living with her aunt in Atlantic City while her parents remained in Teheran.

When word of Miss Bahadori's selection got out, some teachers and parents protested. Ted Manes, a social studies teacher, circulated a petition against the choice of Tina, and almost half the faculty signed it. "It was poor judgment to pick her. They're holding our citizens hostage, and we turn around and honor one of their nationals," said Mr. Manes.

As a result of the outcry, Tina decided to withdraw, and the valedictory address was given by Helene Plotka. Helene told reporters, "I don't like to think that all of this has soured Tina's impression of the United States. The students are supportive of her, and the whole matter is absurd."

The furor continued even after graduation. Some students were shocked at their teachers' behavior; others defended the petition on the grounds that a valedictorian should have been in the school for the full four years; several also pointed out that Miss Bahadori's parents, who were still in Iran, might be in jeopardy over the whole issue.

Presumably, Tina was hurt by the affair, but she refused to criticize the authorities. She had been accepted as a pre-engineering student by the Massachusetts Institute of Technology and was too busy getting ready for college to prolong the controversy.

If debating classes at Atlantic City High ever run short of topics to argue about, they now have a homemade one which should stimulate thought for years to come.

TIME TO REMEMBER AND REFLECT

1. Why were some teachers against the selection of Ms. Bahadori as valedictorian?

2. What did the young Iranian girl do when she heard about the teachers' complaint?

3. What was the new valedictorian's greatest concern about the incident?

4. Why couldn't Ms. Bahadori give too much attention to the problem?

5. What reason did some students offer in support of the teachers' petition?

6. Tell why you agree or disagree with the action taken by those teachers against the selection of the Iranian girl as valedictorian.

7. Helene Plotka, the new valedictorian, said that the students were supportive of Tina Bahadori. What might have happened if they had announced that no one else would agree to serve as valedictorian if Tina were bypassed?

APPOSITIVES, PREDICATE NOMINATIVES, AND RELATIVE CLAUSES

When you have several items of information to impart, you may try a variety of approaches. Assume you have these facts:

The winner of the competition to deliver the valedictory address is Tina Bahadori.

She is a straight *A* student.

She is 18 years old.

She came to this country a year and a half ago.

One method is simply to list the facts as stated. The first three sentences are similarly constructed: subject, verb, predicate nominative. However, this sounds a little childish. You can try other possibilities. You could combine the four sentences into two sentences.

The winner was 18-year-old Tina Bahadori. She is a straight *A* student who came to this country a year and a half ago.

This is better. Your first sentence now uses an adjective (18-year-old) to describe Tina. The second sentence deliberately reduces the importance of the last item by making it a subordinate clause describing the noun *student* (who came to this country...)

There is more you can do. You can combine both these sentences into one with a shorthand method that eliminates the verb *to be* and allows you to insert identifying information immediately after the noun. This method uses the *appositive*, which is discussed further in the Handbook.

The winner, an 18-year-old straight *A* student, was Tina Bahadori, who had come to this country a year and a half ago.

The expression *an 18-year-old straight A student* is an appositive. It provides us with two items of information about the winner, but it is not a sentence because it has no verb. The sentence using this new construction does more than string out the four facts; it presents the information in various forms that indicate the importance you as the writer attach to each item.

81

The major point, the name of the winner, is placed in the position of the predicate nominative, which is on a par with the subject. Next in importance is the clause modifying Tina Bahadori, *who had come to this country a year and a half ago*. Less important still is the fact that she is a straight *A* student, which was made an appositive. Least important is the fact that she is 18 years old, which became a second adjective modifying the appositive *student*. The order of priority is then as follows: main clause, subordinate clause, appositive, adjectives modifying appositive.

The great flexibility of the English language allows you other alternatives:

> The winner, a straight *A* student, was Tina Bahadori, an 18-year-old who came to this country a year and a half ago.

Here the subject, *winner*, is followed by an appositive, *student*, which is modified by the adjective *straight A*. The predicate nominative, *Tina Bahadori*, is also followed by an appositive, which is modified by an adjective clause. The structure here is therefore as follows: subject, adjective, appositive, verb, predicate nominative, appositive, adjective clause. Which version do you prefer? Both are acceptable. Both reflect a mature level of writing.

Following are three sentences from a classic writer on literature, Ford Madox Ford. Note how he used appositives.

> Let us consider Dickens, Balzac, and Thackeray, three novelists all running neck and neck with one another in the matter of time and not singularly different in their approach to life and their works.

The facts dealt with are:

1. Let us consider Dickens, Balzac and Thackeray.
2. These three novelists lived about the same time.
3. They had similar approaches to life.
4. Their works also show similarities.

Sentence 2 was placed in apposition to the writers mentioned in sentence 1. Sentences 3 and 4 were recast into a form that parallels the life and works of the writers. The use of a new sentence was avoided by having the appositive modified by the participle *running* and the adjective *different*. Thus the structure of the sentence is as follows: main clause, appositive with two modifiers.

> There is no reason why Dickens should not have thought himself one of the greatest men in his world or for all time, an epic writer of the scale of Homer; a reformer of the scale of Luther; a great man who had known the poverty of a Villon.

Having said that Dickens regarded himself as one of the greatest men, the writer proceeds to elaborate the thought with three appositives. The first two are each modified by two prepositional phrases; the third is modified by an adjective clause. Admittedly, it takes a while to work up to the stylistic complexity of such a sentence, but once you master the meaning and use of the appositive, you can begin to take a few swipes at more sophisticated writing yourself.

> In the greatest of his books, *Under Western Eyes*, Joseph Conrad analyzed the opposition to the Tzarist regime of his own day in a manner which cast unequalled disdain on the whole Imperial system.

Here the appositive, the title of the novel, is attached to the prepositional phrase that opens the sentence. Can you explain why this preceded the main thought? What subordinate clause ends the sentence?

You have heard that "position is everything in life." This is no less true in writing. In a sentence or in an essay, the beginning and the end get the most attention. In this sentence, Ford used these two key positions, the beginning and the ending, first to identify the book and then to highlight Conrad's attitude towards Russian monarchy.

In summary, to achieve the proper emphasis and nuances in communicating a group of ideas, you as a writer should be aware of:

1. the different grammatical constructions available to you — predicate nominative, appositive, main clause, subordinate clause, modifiers
2. the effect of placement or position within the sentence on the total picture.

YOUR TURN

A. Analyze the structure of the following sentences containing appositives. Tell what is the appositive, what word or words it is in apposition to, and what modifiers (words, phrases, or clauses) are used to further describe the appositive.

1. Industry gobbles up the best high school science teachers, a pool of highly talented, underpaid and often underappreciated people.
2. She remained something of an innocent, a small-town girl filled with feelings of guilt.
3. He names the people who helped tarnish her image — the FBI man, who first proposed the character assassination to his headquarters in Washington; the editor of the *Los Angeles Times*, who fed the gossip columnist Joyce Haber false items.
4. Doctors have noted a decline in the incidence of peptic ulcers, the sores on the lining of the stomach and the small intestines that can cause gnawing pains and can lead to potentially fatal complications.
5. Robert has been accepted in a program for the gifted at PS 153 in Harlem, one of a growing number of cases in which traditional methods of identifying the gifted and talented are being challenged.

B. Combine the following sentences, using appositives.

1. Dr. Brian Brady withdrew his prediction of a major earthquake in Peru and Chile. Dr. Brady is employed by the U.S. Bureau of Mines in Golden, Colorado. Dr. Brady changed his forecast because the seismic activity he had expected had not occurred.
2. Dr. Brady had made his prediction with a colleague. His colleague was Dr. William Spense of the U.S. Geological Survey. Dr. Spense has already declared the earthquake prediction was no longer valid.
3. The inflation rate declined to 6 percent annually in the April to June period. This is its lowest level in more than three years.
4. ABC News scheduled "If You Were the President." It is a special edition of "20/20." It portrays an exercise in White House crisis management. Real players react to the constant twists and dilemmas coping with terrorist incidents.
5. John Steinbeck was opposed to the Horatio Alger myth. That myth praised going "from rags to riches." Steinbeck admired everything that is not a material success. He admired the have-nots, the misfits, the simple, the poor, and the oppressed.

C. Write a paragraph of 200 words on one of the topics below. In your paragraph, be sure to include at least five appositives.

1. The perfect team
2. A day I should have stayed in bed
3. A recent historical event
4. Advice to the ambitious (or lazy)
5. It's easy to bowl (cook, ski, etc.)

For more practice in the use of appositives and predicate nouns, consult the Handbook section on parts of the sentence. Relative clauses are discussed in the section on clauses.

EXPANDING YOUR VOCABULARY

Choose the correct meaning of the italicized words in the sentences. Use the context as a clue.

1. absurd   a) uncertain   b) temporary   c) exaggerated   d) foolish

The students are supportive of her, and the whole matter is *absurd*.

2. circulated   a) demanded   b) composed   c) passed around   d) filed

Ted Manes, a social studies teacher, *circulated* a petition against the choice of Tina.

3. prolong   a) promote   b) continue   c) decide   d) fight
4. controversy   a) misunderstanding   b) argument   c) drama   d) application

She was too busy getting ready for college to *prolong* the *controversy*.

5. furor   a) rage   b) argument   c) fun   d) memory

The *furor* continued even after graduation.

6. hostage   a) guest   b) prisoner   c) incommunicado   d) one held as a pledge that certain promises will be carried out
7. inflamed   a) set afire   b) interrogated   c) made violent   d) held in check
8. militants   a) terrorists   b) warlike people   c) soldiers   d) agents

In 1980 U.S. feelings were *inflamed* because 53 Americans were being held *hostage* by Moslem *militants*.

9. outcry   a) petition   b) pressure   c) demand   d) protest

As a result of the *outcry*, Tina decided to withdraw.

10. valedictory   a) congratulatory   b) opening   c) farewell   d) representative

The top seniors had been invited to compete for the honor of delivering the *valedictory* address at their commencement exercises.

Lesson 24
CHARACTERIZATION

THE LITTLE BROWN BOX

Thomas Morley's trip to New York had been a successful one, and as he entered the taxi-cab outside the St. Moritz Hotel for the ride to the airport, he was relaxed and serene. The little brown box he carried contained fourteen rare coins from the 18th century, which he had purchased in the big city. Once he got back to Cocoa, Florida, those little beauties would become the centerpiece of his collection. He began to mentally rearrange his display cases, trying to decide how to best set off his new treasures.

The taxicab driver, Michael Konaplanik, was more concerned about his head cold than about his passenger, so when Mr. Morley, still planning his display, got out, neither man noticed that the precious box remained on the back seat. Off drove Mr. Konaplanik to nurse his cold while the coin dealer made his way to the airline check-in desk. It wasn't until Mr. Morley had placed his suitcase on the scale that he realized that his $33,000 worth of coins was missing. Frantically, he raced back to the entrance only to discover that the cab was gone.

During the next few hours, Mr. Morley aged rapidly. Because his coins were not insured, he would have to bear the entire loss. Furthermore, he had pursued those particular coins relentlessly for years, and it was cruelly ironic that they would have slipped through his fingers so easily.

The police were summoned. Could Mr. Morley remember the driver's name? Did he recall the license plate number? Was it a company car that they could trace? Mr. Morley's mind was a blank. He had never noticed. The police suggested that he undergo hypnosis in an effort to reconstruct his trip to the airport but that proved fruitless. Believing what he had heard about the evils of the big city, Mr. Morley sat in his hotel room, certain that he would never see his beloved coins again.

Just then, up drove Mr. Konaplanik. While cleaning out his cab he discovered the brown box and returned it immediately to the St. Moritz Hotel. For his honesty, he received the life-long gratitude of an astonished Mr. Morley, as well as a reward of $1000.

"What was all the hullabaloo about?" asked Mr. Konaplanik as he pulled away from the curb. "I find things in my cab every day and always return them. Wouldn't you do the same?"

TIME TO REMEMBER AND REFLECT

1. Why was Mr. Morley so happy during the taxi ride to the airport?

2. Why didn't the taxi driver pay more attention to his passenger during the trip?

3. Why did Mr. Morley feel that he would never see his coins again?

4. What rewards did the taxi driver receive for his honesty?

5. Why was the taxi driver so surprised about the reaction when he returned the coins?

6. If you withdrew $50 from a bank, and the teller gave you $500 by mistake, would you return it? Explain your answer.

7. Mr. Konaplanik received a reward for returning the coins. Is honesty the best policy, therefore?

CHARACTERIZATION

A story usually focuses attention not only on what happened but to whom it happened. In more technical language, we say a story has a plot or series of actions and events that affect one or more characters. These two elements go hand in hand; the reader should have as clear a picture of the people involved in your story as they have of the incidents that befall them.

The careful writer must answer a number of questions about the characters in the tale: How will they look, speak, and act? What do they believe, value, fear? Will they remain the same throughout the story or develop, grow, rise, fall? Of course, the length of the story and the time limits of the writing will determine how much attention is given to character presentation, but no story is complete without it.

Character Development

Even a brief anecdote like "The Little Brown Box" devotes time to character development. We meet Thomas Morley as he is riding in a taxi to the airport, pleased with his purchase of the rare coins. We are given an insight into his state of mind, "relaxed and serene," which will contrast dramatically with his "aging rapidly" when he discovers his loss. Furthermore, the article reveals Mr. Morley's thoughts to us as he reflects contentedly on "those little beauties" which will become the centerpiece of his collection in Cocoa, Florida. This helps us understand his anguish when the coins slip through his fingers. In another short paragraph, Mr. Morley's bitter loss is brought home to us because we actually see him trying desperately to recall the taxi license plate number, submitting to hypnosis to unlock his memory, and finally resigning himself to the sad conclusion that "he would never see his beloved coins again."

Characters As Real People

Mr. Konaplanik too, the hero of the piece, arrives on the scene described with enough detail so we can "see" the character as a flesh and blood human. He is suffering from a head cold — don't we all? He cleans out his cab, as every cabbie does occasionally. As he drives off, $1000 richer, he speaks a line appropriate to his modest nature. "Wouldn't you do the same?" he asks, challenging the reader to match his honesty and somehow making us believe that we know more about this unique man than his few words would ordinarily suggest.

In summary, try to give your characters those touches of speech, dress, appearance, and habit that will both contribute to the story and help the reader think of them as real people.

YOUR TURN

A. In one or two sentences for each, describe the physical appearance of five people, real or fictional, so that a stranger would immediately recognize them in a crowd.

B. Differentiate your characters further by writing about a major trait each of them possesses.

C. Relate an incident which shows one of your characters in action.

D. Write a story of 200 words involving at least three of your characters. Suggestions:

1. All are in pursuit of the same goal.
2. All meet at a vacation resort.
3. All are possible suspects of a crime.
4. All apply for the same job.
5. All find that they are related.

EXPANDING YOUR VOCABULARY

Match the words in Column A with the meanings in Column B.

A	B
1. centerpiece	a. chased
2. frantically	b. condition resembling deep sleep
3. fruitless	c. wildly
4. gratitude	d. uproar; fuss
5. hullabaloo	e. thanks; appreciation
6. hypnosis	f. useless; waste of time
7. pursued	g. calm
8. relentlessly	h. without stop; singlemindedly
9. serene	i. highlight
10. sprinted	j. ran quickly

Lesson 25
MIXING DIFFERENT TECHNIQUES

WOMEN REPORTERS IN MALE LOCKER ROOMS?

When a professional ball game is over, the athletes retreat to their locker rooms to shower and then change into their street clothes. Newspapermen have always used that time for interviews so that they can incorporate the players' reactions into the next day's sports columns. But women reporters, such as Melissa Lincoln of *Sports Illustrated*, were handicapped because club managements prohibited them from entering those traditional sanctuaries thronged with naked athletes.

Ms. Lincoln won a court ruling that mandated that all reporters, regardless of their sex, should have equal access to the locker rooms. The federal judge left the arrangements up to the club managements, pointing out that a short time could be set aside for all interviews, before the players removed their uniforms. Or, if the club wished, the locker room could be barred to all of the media.

A period of confusion followed. Instead of concentrating on the story of the game, reporters were swept up with the excitement of which player strode by which female reporter in what state of undress. Talented women reporters who were serious about their work were exposed to all sorts of criticism as can be seen from the following telephone calls to a radio station:

"Women reporters who go into a men's locker room are just looking to get publicity, not to get a sports story."

"I never thought sex would be injected into pro baseball but I guess the editors feel it will sell newspapers."

"Now a blind woman can get a job as a sportswriter."

Melissa Lincoln, a level-headed young woman, ignores all of the nonsense. She is convinced that her male colleagues have an unfair advantage over her in covering a sports event, and she resents it.

"All that I and other female sportswriters want," she said, "is a chance to compete on an equal level with the men. Without access to the locker room, that is not often possible."

TIME TO REMEMBER AND REFLECT

1. How are the reporters helped by being able to enter the locker rooms after a game?

2. What was the result of Ms. Lincoln's victory in court?

3. What criticism of women reporters did one of the telephone callers make?

4. What magazine does Ms. Lincoln work for?

5. What can the club owners do if they are unhappy about allowing women reporters to enter their locker rooms?

6. "I don't care about what's said in the locker room," a fan said. "Just tell me about the ball game." Is that your sentiment? Why?

7. In what other fields can women point to unfair competition? Are there any fields where women have an unfair advantage over their male rivals?

COMPOSITION POTPOURRI

While we have tried to make clear that each type of writing has its own format, rules and techniques, you should not assume that compositions are an either/or proposition, that your piece must be either narrative or descriptive, expository or argumentative. In fact, you will hardly ever be that strictly limited. A story is mixed with description; persuasion requires at least some explanation. Narrations, descriptions, expositions, dialogues, questions, conclusions — the entire gamut of the writing techniques discussed in this text — frequently appear in a mixture that makes it difficult to identify even the major element. Hence, it is important to keep in mind all the principles pertaining to the varieties of composition types and use each to the best advantage.

An All-Purpose Approach

The selection "Women Reporters in Male Locker Rooms" is a good illustration of a multi-faceted yet effective piece of writing. The first paragraph begins with a description of what happens after an athletic event and a statement of the problem faced by women reporters. This is followed by a narrative portion that records the court ruling calling for equal access by all reporters, male and female, to interview the athletes. Next comes a section of description – narration – exposition with an editorial tinge, culminating in a series of quotations from telephone callers expressing their views of the new turn of events. Finally, the article concludes with a calm statement by the level-headed plaintiff, Melissa Lincoln, who makes her pitch for equal treatment. No shrill arguments, no beating the drums, no histrionics. Just plain talk that comes straight to the point. Sometimes the best argument may be the simplest and the most straightforward.

YOUR TURN

A. Review the major approaches in writing (a) description (b) a narration (c) an exposition (d) an argument.

B. Select a recent article from *Vital Speeches*, *Reader's Digest*, a newspaper, or magazine of your own choosing and comment on the highlights: purpose, point of view, methods and devices, organization, conclusion.

C. Select from any source a story or article you enjoyed and admired. Tell specifically what you like about it and why. Then keep these features in mind as you write a similar piece, using the selection as your model.

EXPANDING YOUR VOCABULARY

Choose the correct meaning of the italicized words in the sentences. Use the context as a clue.

1. mandated   a) permitted   b) denied   c) ordered   d) suggested
2. access   a) practice   b) inside information   c) entry   d) surplus

Ms. Lincoln won a court ruling which *mandated* that all reporters, regardless of their sex, should have equal *access* to locker rooms.

3. incorporate   a) clarify   b) insert   c) combine with something   d) quote
4. reactions   a) comments   b) moods   c) excuses   d) ideas

Newspapermen have always used that time for interviews so that they might *incorporate* the players' *reactions* into the next day's sports columns.

5. media   a) fans   b) visitors   c) public   d) representatives of the press

Or, if the club wished, the locker room could be barred to all of the *media*.

6. prohibited   a) prevented   b) limited   c) advised   d) monitored
7. sanctuaries   a) hiding places   b) public places   c) protected places   d) uncharted places
8. thronged   a) decorated   b) crowded   c) off limits   d) praised

But women reporters were handicapped because club managements *prohibited* them from entering those traditional *sanctuaries* which were *thronged* with naked athletes.

9. retreat   a) surrender   b) run   c) relax   d) move back

When a professional ball game is over, the athletes *retreat* to their locker rooms.

10. segment   a) pep talk   b) angle   c) section   d) review

The federal judge left the arrangements up to the club managements, pointing out that a short *segment* could be set aside for all interviews before the players removed their uniforms.

Lesson 26
PERSUASION

OUTSIDE THE LAW

In a recent movie, a character's wife was killed by some neighborhood hoodlums. He set about to avenge her death by exposing himself to attacks in parks and on desolate streets — and then shot his assailants before they could do their dirty work. For his vigilante work, the character was cheered lustily by audiences who were happy to see a private citizen striking back at those culprits whom the police could not control.

In South America, that kind of action against criminals is well known. Since 1964, "death squads" of Rio de Janeiro police, who call themselves the White Hand, have accounted for the executions of thousands of suspected murderers, drug dealers, thieves, and rapists. While the authorities have condemned this orgy of lawlessness, the public applauds it because they feel that conventional justice moves too slowly and ineffectually to help them.

White Hand members, wearing stocking masks, have broken into the homes of known criminals just before dawn. After dragging those men from their beds and shooting them, the White Hand then calls the police station to tell the officials where the bodies are.

Yet in their search for quick justice, the White Hand representatives have committed serious injustices, their critics complain. An innocent house painter opened his door to explain to a White Hand team that the thief they were seeking did not live in his house — but he was cut down by a staccato blast of gun fire before he could tell his story.

TIME TO REMEMBER AND REFLECT

1. What led the character to become a vigilante in the movie?

2. Why was his vigilante work applauded so enthusiastically by movie audiences?

3. To which large organization do the "death squads" belong?

4. Why haven't the families of the executed criminals been able to identify the vigilantes?

5. What evidence is there that the "death squads" have committed injustices?

6. If you lived in South America, would you applaud the activities of the death squads? Why?

7. Justice should be quick, punishment of guilty persons should be certain. Why, then, are lawmen critical of the death squads?

PERSUASION

The art of Persuasion is a critical skill that demands more preparation and care than other forms of writing. Perhaps that is only fair and proper, since winning someone over to your point of view is generally more important than narrating a story, describing a scene, or even explaining a process. Often you are trying to persuade people not only to agree with you but to follow through with an action. In such a case you must think carefully so that you can present your case clearly and honestly.

What are the basic principles of this skill? We can find some of them illustrated in the selection "Outside the Law." Few rational people would agree that we should take the law into our own hands. One risk is obvious: abuse by ruthless individuals or groups can lead to anarchy. But if we are first told of a movie in which the hero seeks to avenge the death of his wife, killed by mindless young punks, we can sympathize with his feelings. When the hero launches a one-man campaign against muggers and hoodlums and turns the tables on those who terrorize decent citizens, we may even applaud his actions with enthusiasm. The writer has thus established a common ground, a point of sympathy and agreement. The stage is now set for the next step, to real, not fictional, lawlessness.

Once we have accepted the actions of the movie hero, we may be ready to condone the White Hand death squads, who exercise private judgment and punish suspected criminals without recourse to the police and the courts. Accounts of typical attacks are given in the story you read. Known criminals are summarily executed without benefit— or delays— of the law.

But the selection ends with a sober note. Not always is swift and certain punishment the answer. Indeed, as the story of the innocent house painter graphically demonstrates, it may even lead to a tragic miscarriage of justice.

USEFUL GROUND RULES

Here, then, are some ground rules for a solid persuasive composition: The introduction to an argument should be clear as to the topic and your point of view.
You may be direct:

> The United Nations organization has not fulfilled its purpose.

Or you may be subtle:

> Hardly a year has passed since the founding of the United Nations without a serious flare up in some part of the world. Hunger, disease, pollution, discrimination, terrorism, and revolution are rampant. The major powers are engaged in a spiralling arms race. Inflation, bankruptcies and oil prices are on the rise while standards of living and confidence in the future are plummeting. The threat of a nuclear holocaust hovers over us. Can we truly say our world is a safer, happier place for mankind now that the United Nations is here?

When you follow up your thesis with accurate facts and powerful reasons, you are scoring points. When you use examples, illustrations, statistics, or recognized authorities to strengthen your argument, you are scoring points. When you hit upon just the right word or phrase that will tug at the heartstrings or strike a sympathetic chord, that too is a perfectly legitimate use of language to persuade — as long as you do not depend solely on an emotional appeal. Remember that people are moved by appeals to the head and the heart.

Don't forget that in persuasion it is entirely proper not only to build your arguments but also to point out the weaknesses of opposing views. In other words, to convince people you must be doubly prepared to show how solidly built your argument is, and how shaky your opponent's is.

Examples Help

Let's look at the "mortar and brick" that will build your case into an impregnable structure. First is the use of examples. Find an instance where your plan was applied and it worked. Show that your candidate succeeded in the past in the kind of job he is now running for.

Using Statistics

Citing statistics is also an effective way of fortifying your argument. With statistics you are saying that your viewpoint is true for many people, many occasions, many times and places. Of course, you cannot simply make up the figures. You must either collect the data yourself or find it in reliable publications. Be sure to mention your sources and give the proper credit.

Quotations from Experts

Closely related to statistics are the quotations from experts in the subject you are examining. A statement from the mayor on a political issue, from a successful businessman on an economic plan, from a famous sports figure on the importance of training will go a long way to prove that yours is not a half-baked opinion. But be careful. That sports figure may be a good authority on training, but not on the value of an economic plan. Your authorities must be people who can be expected to know what they are talking about.

Accurate Description

Finally, you may be arguing a point that is best proven by describing exactly what would happen, as accurately as you can predict, if your view is adopted. Be fair and honest. Follow your idea to its logical conclusion to persuade the reader that it would make sense, be worthwhile, bring substantial benefits or advantages. If you are arguing for or against more conservation to solve the energy problem, more policemen to deter crime, strengthening of the social security system, or outlawing of handguns, paint a detailed picture of the situation should your view prevail. The advantages — or disadvantages—should be made crystal clear.

Strong Ending

Caution! You are not finished persuading until you have delivered the final punch, a strong ending. Don't walk away from the argument without restating your basic position. This may be done by paraphrasing the topic sentence, mentioning again your most emphatic point, summarizing briefly a number of reasons, or asking a rhetorical question that will leave the reader thinking or ready to act.

YOUR TURN

Use the topics listed—or one of your own choosing—to complete the assignments below.

Topics:

1. Diets are a waste of time and energy
2. Advertisements are out to fool the unwary
3. Movies (or TV shows or sports) are better than ever
4. The jeans craze proves American gullibility
5. We are too easy on criminals
6. Capital punishment would deter crime
7. _____ is the best (actor, actress, athlete, singer) today

8. _____ is the up-and-coming sport
9. The future belongs to _____
10. Today's schools are a failure
11. Space exploration should be discontinued
12. The UN should be abolished

Assignments: (You may take either side of an argument.)

1. Write a sentence that states your point of view clearly and effectively.
2. Write an introduction designed to win over a hostile audience to your side. (Find a common ground.)
3. Use a forceful comparison to prove a point.

4. Refute an argument that might possibly be brought up by your opponent.
5. Make a purely emotional appeal for one side of an issue.
6. Write a strong concluding sentence on one of the topics.
7. Write a well-organized, three-paragraph composition of 250 words on the topic you feel most strongly about. Use as many techniques as you can muster for your argument. Once again, review the three-paragraph essay suggestions that follow "Dr. Shanna," Lesson 5.

EXPANDING YOUR VOCABULARY

Match the words in Column A with the meanings in Column B.

A	B
1. avenge	a. customary
2. conventional	b. get even
3. culprit	c. deserted
4. desolate	d. gangsters
5. exposing	e. vigorously
6. hoodlums	f. ordinary; usual
7. ineffectually	g. wild participation; overindulgence
8. lustily	h. lawbreaker
9. orgy	i. uselessly
10. staccato	j. abrupt

Lesson 27
CHOOSING A TITLE

I BEFORE E, EXCEPT AFTER C

ROY G. BIV.

"Spring ahead, fall back"

HOMES

You may have trouble making sense out of the above lines, but they have been most beneficial to millions of people. To put it simply, they are mnemonic (memory) devices. In ROY G. BIV each letter stands for a color of the visible spectrum: red, orange, yellow, green, blue, indigo, violet. "Spring ahead, fall back" helps us to remember that in the spring we turn our clocks ahead one hour, while in the fall we reverse the process. And the five letters in HOMES have assisted many crossword puzzle fans to recall the names of the Great Lakes: *H*uron, *O*ntario, *M*ichigan, *E*rie, and *S*uperior.

Pupils studying for tests have used such memory devices to good advantage. If there are fifteen crucial items to recollect, it is possible to take their first letters and organize them into a catchy word or phrase and then impress a teacher with that comprehensive knowledge.

Future doctors who have had to learn long lists of nerves and bones in order to pass their medical school exams have become quite skillful with mnemonic devices. For example: *On old Olympus' towering top, a fat armed German vaults and hops* translates into twelve cranial nerves: *o*lfactory, *o*ptic, *o*culomotor, *t*rochlear, *t*rigeminal, *a*bducents, *f*acial, *a*coustic, *g*lossopharyngeal, *v*agus, *a*ccessory, *h*ypoglossal.

Students of American history who want to be able to tick off all of our presidents in order will find that the first letters of this forty-one word jingle will do the trick for them:

"Washington and Jefferson made many a joke, Van Buren had to put the frying pan back, Lincoln just gasped, 'Heaven guard America.' Cleveland had coats made ready to wear home, Coolidge hurried right to every kitchen jar's neck for cookie raisins."

The next time someone challenges you to name the planets in order from the sun, merely conjure up, "My very earnest mother just served us nine pickles," and you will have successfully listed the clues to Mercury, Venus, Earth, Mars, Jupiter, Saturn, Uranus, Neptune, and Pluto.

Some people are critical of memory devices, saying that they do not represent true learning. But to the person who could never recall the difference between stalagmites and stalactites until he learned "The mites go up, the tights go down," mnemonic devices are a blessing.

TIME TO REMEMBER AND REFLECT

1. What code word will help someone to remember the names of the five Great Lakes?

2. According to the article, why might a medical student profit a great deal from memory devices?

3. How can we be helped to remember whether to move our clocks forward or back in the springtime?

4. Of what use is it to remember "the mites go up, the tights go down"?

5. We all know that George Washington was the first president; how can we tell, from the article, what number Ronald Reagan was?

6. Some teachers are very critical of pupils who rely on mnemonic devices, feeling that they are substituting artificial learning for true learning. Tell why you agree or disagree with those critics.

7. Take an important set of names from one of your study areas and arrange it in the form of a mnemonic device.

CHOOSING A TITLE: WHAT SHALL I CALL IT?

"What's in a name?" Shakespeare has Juliet ask. "That which we call a rose by any other name would smell as sweet." Romeo and Juliet felt that way because they knew and loved each other, and their names only reminded them of the long-standing feuds between their families. However, the writer who has yet to woo and win the reader's attention must rely heavily on a title or name that is catchy, appealing, beguiling, inviting, intriguing, and enticing. What's in a name? Plenty. Without the right title, the reader might not even glance at your efforts. It is the doorway through which the reader enters your world and follows the ideas you have painstakingly gathered. You must try at all costs to make an impression in your first contact with the reader — your title.

Titles can be precise, stating exactly what your composition will discuss. Titles can reveal something of your viewpoint as well as the subject matter. Titles should follow these guidelines:

1. They should whet the appetite of the reader but not reveal too much.
2. They should not promise more or less than the writing actually delivers, or, to put it differently, they should not give a false or misleading impression.
3. They should usually be short or you run the danger that a reader will pass right over them.
4. They should not be too general or indefinite, as "An Adventure," "A Friend," or "My Opinion of Politicians."
5. They should not be giveaways, such as "Saved by the Telephone."

The Right Title

Let us consider the selection titled "I Before E, Except After C." This title uses a spelling rule known to most students and hopes to snare your attention by appealing to the familiar. At the same time, a quick glance will reveal that the article is not about spelling after all. What then was the author's purpose in choosing this title? Perhaps the spelling rule is only an example of the kind of information to be found in this piece. You reason, "Since I know the title refers to a useful rule, I can expect other helpful hints on various topics." Once you have been stimulated to think about the article, to wonder, and to anticipate, the title has done its work. You're hooked.

YOUR TURN

A. Find a book of essays or short stories and select five appealing titles. Be prepared to explain why you chose them.

B. Make up titles for stories or compositions suggested by five of the following: friends, dancing, bridges, teachers, dating, vacations, patriotism, boxing, medicines, accidents.

C. Cut out five pictures from newspapers or magazines. Write two titles for each, stressing different aspects of the picture. Compare with the title or caption that came with the picture.

D. Compose alternate titles to match or top the titles for the selections in this text.

EXPANDING YOUR VOCABULARY

Choose the correct meaning of the italicized words in the sentences. Use the context as a clue.

1. cranial   a) related to the spine   b) skull   c) muscles   d) bones
2. acoustic   a) related to talking   b) hearing   c) seeing   d) breathing

"On old Olympus' towering top, a fat armed German vaults and hops" translates into the 12 *cranial* nerves: olfactory, optic, oculomotor, trochlear, trigeminal, abducents, facial, *acoustic*, glossopharyngeal, vagus, accessory, hypoglossal.

3. beneficial   a) favoring   b) expensive   c) useful   d) comforting

You may have trouble making sense out of the above lines but they have been most *beneficial* to millions of people.

4. crucial   a) secret   b) scholarly   c) imaginative   d) of the highest importance
5. comprehensive   a) selective   b) thorough   c) available   d) unforgettable

If there are 15 *crucial* items to recollect, it is possible to take their first letters and organize them into a catchy word or phrase and then impress a teacher with that *comprehensive* knowledge.

6. conjure up   a) summon   b) announce   c) remember   d) hypnotize

The next time someone challenges you to name the planets in order from the sun, merely *conjure up* "My very earnest mother just served us nine pickles," and you will have successfully listed the clues to Mercury, Venus, Earth, Mars, Jupiter, Saturn, Uranus, Neptune, and Pluto.

7. recall   a) send back   b) remember   c) memory   d) explain

To the person who could never *recall* the difference between stalagmites and stalactites until he learned "The mites go up, the tights go down," mnemonic devices are a blessing.

8. reverse   a) repeat   b) change   c) modify   d) go back

In the fall we *reverse* the process.

9. visible   a) adjustable   b) illuminated   c) able to be seen   d) definite
10. spectrum   a) horizon   b) universe   c) arrangement of colored bands   d) canvas

Each letter stands for a color of the *visible spectrum*.

Lesson 28
HUMOR AND IRONY

OPENING A CAN OF WORMS

Every day, the Department of Taxation and Finance in Albany, New York's capital city, receives anonymous tips about businessmen who are evading the payment of sales taxes. Routinely, form letters are then sent to those merchants, asking for details about their sales and profits. In some instances, however, agents are dispatched to make a surprise investigation of the business and to verify the allegations.

That brings us to the case of Jody Gerard. Last summer he got a certified letter about unpaid taxes. It contained a threatening statement to the effect that if he didn't pay up within 20 days, New York State would be forced to take punitive action against him and his company. Since that could have meant the loss of his profitable business, Jody secured a state sales tax license and sent in the complete payment of what he owed—64 cents!

You see, Jody Gerard is only 12 years old, and has been selling worms to fishermen. He digs them up in his backyard in Eddyville, New York and charges 35 cents a dozen for the red wriggling beauties.

When the tax agents swooped down on Jody's tiny enterprise, their faces were red:

"We had no idea it was a 12-year-old boy. If we had, it would have been handled differently. After all, we've got better things to do with our time than to raid every kiddy lemonade stand in the state."

Nevertheless, until legislation is passed to exempt fuzzy-cheeked entrepreneurs from paying sales tax, they will have to do so. Since the law cracked down on Jody Gerard, however, his business has become so popular that he can hardly find enough worms to satisfy the tourists.

When the tax people started to throw their weight around, Jody's mother was really angry. Now she sees some educational merit in the incident:

"At least my boy has already learned that he will have to pay taxes for the rest of his life."

TIME TO REMEMBER AND REFLECT

1. How did the tax agents learn about Jody Gerard?

2. What did the Department of Taxation and Finance want the young boy to do? How much money did Jody actually owe?

3. Where was Jody's source of supply for his customers?

4. What effect did all of the publicity have on his worm business? What will that mean in terms of his future dealings with the state?

5. What value did Mrs. Gerard see for her son in this episode?

6. Do you approve of the system of rewarding citizens who inform the government about tax cheats? Why?

7. Tax experts claim that our city, state, and federal governments lose billions of dollars each year because people cheat on their taxes. Suggest several specific ways in which our officials can do a better job of collecting the money that is legitimately owed.

HUMOR AND IRONY

Humor is often attained by exaggeration, called *hyperbole* in technical language. When you say, "I'm so hungry I could eat a horse," or "I worked so hard yesterday I came home absolutely dead," or "Some people love to chew your ears off with gossip," you obviously don't mean them literally, but such expressions help you get your point across.

Another approach in communicating your ideas effectively, *irony*, goes even further: you say the exact opposite of what you mean, but the true meaning is so clear that you can be sure your words will not be misinterpreted. For example, if you have invested time and money preparing for a picnic with your friends, and the eagerly awaited day arrives accompanied by a thunderous storm, you comment sadly, "How about this beautiful weather?" In the circumstances, no one would take your description literally. You are obviously being ironic.

Irony at Work

In conversation, your sarcastic tone will let the listener know that you are using irony. In writing you must be sure to include enough explanation so that your irony will not be lost or misunderstood. Be sure there is enough of a "gap" between the subject and your treatment. For example, irony is present in describing the efforts of a waddling hippopotamus to move through the mud as "dainty." Do you see the incongruity? That is a proper use of irony.

Humor

Another technique is to underplay or tone down a subject, adopting a tongue-in-cheek approach. Understatement is illustrated in the story of the Englishman who was being consoled by an acquaintance.

"Sorry you buried your wife today."

"Had to. Dead, you know."

Our story "Opening a Can of Worms" employs irony to achieve humor. It starts with a statement about that august institution, the Department of Taxation and Finance, much feared and respected by the average citizen, particularly around April 15. Reference is made to routine mail checks of businesses suspected of trying to evade taxes and even an occasional surprise visit by special investigators. The second paragraph holds us in suspense for just a little longer until we learn that 12-year-old Jody's "business" of selling worms to fishermen was in arrears to the U.S. Government to the tune of 64 cents. Understandably, the tax agents who swooped down on Jody's enterprise developed an immediate case of red-faced embarrassment. There is further irony in the story in that as a result of the raid by the revenue collectors, Jody's worm business really got off the ground and was flying high.

There you have irony — for effect, for style, and for fun. And the wonder of it is that you have succeeded in making your point by intentionally hiding or disguising the truth.

Your Turn

A. Describe the following situations in two ways: first, use a matter-of-fact approach, putting the events in proper perspective; and then, use hyperbole, and exaggerate their importance or consequences.

1. Losing your first baby tooth
2. Being jilted
3. First date
4. A bad purchase
5. A scolding received for a trivial offense

B. Stretch your imagination! Describe what would be impossible except in your wildest dreams. Complete the following with the most outrageous exaggerations you can think of:

1. It was so hot that...
2. Mike is so greedy that...
3. I never come late but today...
4. My neighbor is so strange that...

C. Now try your hand at irony. Make a statement about each of the following that says the opposite of what you mean:

Example: Burly George has just beaten his opponent to a pulp. You say: George, you know, wouldn't hurt a fly.

1. Your car broke down for the nineteenth time this week.
2. Brian thinks he's God's gift to the fair sex.
3. Your friends partied at your house last night and left it in shambles.
4. Your team ran its losing streak to 28, a world record.
5. You've just had the misfortune of bumping into a police car.

D. Write a story of 200 words using irony and/or hyperbole to convey your feelings or mood. Suggested topics:

1. A piece of cake
2. A dime
3. A mysterious caller
4. A routine day
5. Disaster on the home front

EXPANDING YOUR VOCABULARY

Match the words in Column A with the meanings in Column B.

A	B
1. allegations	a. business; project
2. anonymous	b. to free from
3. dispatched	c. business organizers and managers
4. enterprise	d. to make sure
5. entrepreneur	e. charges; accusations
6. evading	f. concerned with punishment
7. exempt	g. sent
8. merit (n)	h. escaping; avoiding doing something
9. punitive	i. unsigned
10. verify	j. worth; value

Lesson 29
ALLUSIONS

CHEATING ON TESTS

You are taking a test in biology, a subject which has always been your nemesis. You are working your way through the labyrinth of questions when a student near the front of the room asks the teacher to explain an item on the question sheet. The teacher is not Janus-faced and as he turns his back on the entire class while he leans over to help, you have more than a minute to safely sneak a look at a classmate's paper. What do you do?

The algebra teacher is lazy and lethargic. She gives your fifth period class the same test that her second period students took. You have an opportunity to get the questions in advance from a friend in the earlier group. What do you do?

An educational assistant is proctoring your social studies test while the regular teacher is in the library entering report card grades. It might be easy to flip open your notebook and get the answers to the questions on dates and inventions because the educational assistant seems to be perusing a newspaper — or is it a Trojan Horse situation and the minute you make a wrong move, the proctor will swoop down on you like a harpy? What do you do?

Over 2000 readers responded to a recent column which psychologist Ellis Sloane writes for a Midwestern newspaper syndicate. Some told of guilt feelings when they cheated on school tests; others had no compunction about lifting an answer from a neighbor's paper; some blamed their parents for pressuring them to get high marks; a few wrote about the need to pass their subjects in order to remain eligible for athletics; several said that their parents had set poor examples for them by openly cheating on their income taxes. Many wanted to know why they had to be pure when "everyone else was knee-deep in cheating."

Dr. Sloane discovered that the majority of pupils will cheat if they can get away with it. "The opportunity to cheat," he said "becomes their Achilles' heel." He found that when careless teachers present the temptation, most youngsters will succumb to it. In such cases, according to Dr. Sloane, "the teacher deserves to be flunked." Despite occasional references to parental values, the psychologist concluded that "the teachers are the determining factor when it comes to children cheating in school."

Prof. Gerard B. Oak, a noted educational consultant, has also placed a large part of the blame for cheating on teachers' shoulders: "It's every teacher's responsibility to make up challenging but fair exams, and then to proctor them so diligently that no student can ever get the chance to cheat. Looking out the window when you should be proctoring alertly is just as ridiculous as assigning the fox to guard the chickens."

TIME TO REMEMBER AND REFLECT

1. How did the algebra teacher's laziness encourage some students to cheat?

2. According to the letters which Dr. Sloane received, what would most students have done when their biology teacher turned his back on the class?

3. In the article, what two reasons involving their parents did some people offer for cheating on school tests?

4. Based on what Dr. Oak said, would he recommend that an alcoholic be given a job as a bartender? Why?

5. Where did Dr. Sloane place the greatest blame for cheating?

6. In your opinion, what is the most important reason why students try to cheat on tests? If every course at your school had a Pass/Fail mark, instead of a numerical grade, would that reduce the amount of cheating? Why?

7. A teacher noted that his advanced students were more likely to cheat than were his remedial students. Assuming that to be true as a general observation, how can you explain it?

ALLUSIONS

Writing should be simple and direct. Yet there are times when a carefully chosen reference to history or literature can make a point clear. Suppose you are discussing a football game in which the quarterback deftly wards off several tacklers and throws a 50-yard touchdown pass. What better word than *herculean* to describe his effort? But this assumes you know that Hercules was a demi-god or hero in Greek mythology who was given superhuman tasks to perform. Now any tremendously difficult undertaking is called "herculean." A literary allusion of this type will add depth and precision to your writing.

Take a look at some of the allusions used in the selection "Cheating on Tests." "Biology has always been your nemesis." Nemesis was the goddess of punishment, especially bringing down the proud. It now means something or someone that inevitably causes defeat or frustration. If that is how the writer feels about biology, does it not make the opportunity to cheat more tempting?

Consider the "labyrinth of questions." The labyrinth was an intricate network of winding passages where the fabled Minotaur was kept, appeased by an annual human sacrifice. Once inside the labyrinth, the hapless victims, unable to find their way out, fell prey to the voracious half-man, half-bull. Do you see why the writer regarded the test as a labyrinth of questions?

Mythology as a Source

Similar stories are attached to *lethargic, Janus-faced, Trojan Horse, harpy,* and *Achilles' heel,* all derived from Greek or Roman mythology. And, lest you think this is the only type of allusion, you will find at the end of the selection a reference to the fox guarding the chickens, which is taken from folklore. In fact, allusions from all sources — history, literature, the Bible, fables, mythology of all nations — will enrich your writing by adding substance and known quantities to help express the ideas you are groping for.

Allusions can be as old as Adam and Eve or as modern as Superman, as crazy as the Mad Hatter or as somber as the Stygian darkness, as plentiful as a cornucopia or as cold and dead as Niflheim. Whatever you want to say has in all likelihood some counterpart in the great and noble voices of the past.

YOUR TURN

A. Explain three of the allusions from each of the fields below.

B. Write sentences with five allusions from each group.

C. Write a paragraph of 200 words in which you include at least ten allusions.

History	Literature	Bible and Religion
Napoleon	the Holy Grail	Methusaleh
Paul Revere's ride	Mr. Micawber	David and Jonathan
Caesar	the Hunchback of Notre Dame	Beelzebub
Black Death	Excalibur	Sermon on the Mount
Bill of Rights	Hamlet	leviathan
Spartan	quixotic	Solomon
D-Day	Don Juan	Buddha
Utopian	Sherlock Holmes	jeremiad
Machiavellian	falstaffian	Sodom and Gomorrah
gerrymander	malapropism	manna

Mythology	Fables and Folklore	Miscellaneous Allusions
Damon and Pythias	Robin Hood	spoonerism
phoenix	fox and the crow	model-T
Medusa	Open Sesame	Picasso
Martian	the river Jordan	Einstein
Elysian Fields	Baron Munchhausen	lese majesty
Tantalus	the Flying Dutchman	mesmerize
Thor	the riddle of the Sphinx	Iron Curtain
Procrustean	Arabian Nights	stoic
Promethean	the Pony Express	Blarney Stone
Happy Hunting Grounds	Paul Bunyan	natural selection

EXPANDING YOUR VOCABULARY

Choose the correct meaning of the italicized words in the sentences. Use the context as a clue.

1. compunction   a) fear   b) sense of guilt   c) opportunity   d) need

Others had no *compunction* about lifting an answer from a neighbor's paper.

2. determining   a) deciding   b) only   c) working   d) probable
3. factor   a) person   b) division   c) reason   d) circumstance

The teachers are the *determining factor* when it comes to children cheating in school.

4. eligible   a) interested   b) allowed to participate   c) rewarded   d) chosen

A few wrote about the need to pass the subjects in order to remain *eligible* for athletics.

5. perusing   a) marking up   b) folding   c) skimming   d) reading carefully

The educational assistant seems to be *perusing* a newspaper.

103

6. proctoring   a) studying   b) distributing   c) supervising   d) collecting

An educational assistant is *proctoring* your social studies test while the regular teacher is in the library entering report card grades.

7. syndicate   a) contest   b) university   c) conference   d) organization

Over 2000 readers responded to a recent newspaper column which psychologist Ellis Sloane writes for a midwestern newspaper *syndicate*.

8. temptation   a) instruction   b) invitation to do something you shouldn't   c) justification   d) wrong attitude

9. succumb   a) ignore   b) give in   c) fail   d) justify

He found that when careless teachers present the *temptation*, most youngsters will *succumb* to it.

10. lethargic   a) annoyed   b) unfair   c) drowsy   d) unfriendly

The algebra teacher is lazy and *lethargic*.

Lesson 30
DIALOGUE

THE REVOLT OF HELEN

The scene is a real estate office in Seattle, Washington where a new secretary is busy transcribing the dictation which she had taken from several of the rental agents. The boss calls out to her, "Helen, would you mind making us a fresh pot of coffee?"

"Sorry, Mr. Hawkins, you'll have to do that yourself."

Mr. Hawkins, who had a low boiling point and was not used to having his subordinates refuse to carry out his orders, insisted that she make the coffee.

"Our secretaries always make coffee," he sputtered.

"As much as I like the job," Helen replied, "if you tell me that I have to serve you coffee, I quit." And she did!

Complications set in when Helen applied for unemployment benefits. The officials turned her down, claiming that she had left her job voluntarily, without good cause, and was not entitled to receive weekly unemployment checks. Helen decided to appeal the case, and a State Labor Department administrative law judge ruled in her favor:

"Her resignation was with good cause. An employee is not required to get coffee for her supervisor unless it is explained to her at the time of hiring that it would be one of her job duties."

The head of the local chapter of N.O.W. (National Organization for Women) was ecstatic about the verdict: "A job is a job and you shouldn't be asked to cut your boss's toenails. Women employees deserve to be treated with respect."

Helen is slated to receive $2025 in retroactive benefits, as well as be eligible for $115 a week for the remainder of her 26 week unemployment period. She has also filed a complaint of sex discrimination with the State Human Rights Commission.

"Mr. Hawkins called it a woman's place to get coffee. I call that downright chauvinism!"

Our scene now shifts to a large department store. The manager has summoned five of his buyers (four men and a woman) to stay for an emergency dinner meeting in his office. He is about to ask the lone woman to set out the sandwiches and drinks...

TIME TO REMEMBER AND REFLECT

1. What was Helen doing when her boss asked her to make the coffee?

2. Why couldn't Helen collect unemployment benefits at first?

3. Who said, "Her resignation was with good cause"?

4. Why was the head of the National Organization for Women's chapter so pleased with Helen's victory?

5. What other action did Helen take against her former boss?

6. Making coffee isn't such a burdensome task. Should Helen have done it — or was she right in quitting the job? Explain.

7. Helen labeled her boss's action as "chauvinism." Look that word up in a dictionary if you are unfamiliar with it and then tell of an incident in which someone you know was guilty of chauvinism.

DIALOGUE

One sure-fire way of perking up a narrative piece is to let the reader or listener hear exactly what is being said. Rather than report that Helen refused to get her boss some coffee, the writer lets us eavesdrop on the conversation: "Sorry, Mr. Hawkins, you'll have to do that yourself." The difference is significant. We are not simply told in an indirect, second-hand way what was said. We are right there, listening, hearing every word directly and judging for ourselves the effect. That is the advantage of dialogue.

Indeed, one form of literature uses dialogue exclusively to tell a story. That is a play or drama, the oldest and perhaps still the most popular form of entertainment. Movies, television, plays and operas all base their appeal to some degree on the fact that we like to hear what people in various circumstances are saying to each other.

Springboard to Fame

A story is told of a reporter at a trial who accidentally gained instant fame by resorting to dialogue. He had stepped out of the courtroom during a crucial moment. Upon his return he found that the reporters for the rival newspapers were busy digesting, summarizing, and rewriting the statements of the lawyers and witnesses. Not having the time to write the usual story, he decided to send to his newspaper the exact words of the speakers as they appeared in the court records, hoping his editors would do the rewriting. But the dialogue, as it came across the wires, needed no rewriting and the editor scooped the other papers by printing the dialogue exactly as he had received it.

Dialogue — with its faults of poor grammar or dialect or repetitions, hemming and hawing — is still closer to the truth than someone's interpretation of what a speaker said or meant.

Appropriateness of the Dialogue

In writing dialogue, remember to keep a speaker's words in line with his or her age, education, and social and economic background, as well as with the requirements of the story — moving the narrative along, showing what a person is thinking, making the situation more interesting and realistic. Remember, too, to punctuate dialogue according to the following rules:

1. Use quotation marks to set off a character's words:

"Our secretaries always make coffee," he sputtered.

The boss calls out, "Helen, would you mind making us a fresh pot of coffee?"

2. If a sentence of dialogue is interrupted by tag words (he said, she replied, etc.) do not begin the second part of the dialogue with a capital letter:

"As much as I like the job," Helen replied, "if you tell me that I have to serve you coffee, I quit."

The word *if* is not capitalized because it is not a new sentence spoken by Helen. It is a continuation of the sentence beginning *As much as*....The words *Helen replied* are tag words or interrupters and are not part of the speech. The Handbook section on quotations (page 151) provides more practice in punctuating dialogue.

YOUR TURN

A. Use a Thesaurus to find at least ten interesting synonyms for *said*. Write a sentence appropriate for each synonym: Billy whimpered, "Why can't I have my dessert now?"

B. Record verbatim (or as closely as possible) a 150-200 word conversation you heard at home, at work, at school, in the street, in the cafeteria, in the pool, or on the playing field.

C. Use dialogue to write a short narrative about one of the following events:

1. A senior discusses a choice of career or college with a parent.
2. An employee tries to explain his third lateness in a week.
3. A storekeeper wants to sell you a "bargain."
4. You call your girlfriend/boyfriend to break a date.
5. A teacher informs a student that he/she is failing.

D. Write 3 different versions of the same incident (it may be one of the above) changing the age, sex, or social background of the main characters.

EXPANDING YOUR VOCABULARY

Match the words in Column A with the meanings in Column B.

A	B
1. chauvinism	a. joyful
2. complications	b. back; covering an earlier time
3. discrimination	c. those of lower rank
4. ecstatic	d. talked in an explosive manner
5. retroactive	e. scheduled
6. slated	f. tangles; confusions
7. sputtered	g. making a copy
8. subordinates	h. bad treatment; prejudice
9. transcribing	i. decision; judgment
10. verdict	j. exaggerated pride in one's own group

Part II
Your Language Handbook

- Parts of Speech
- Punctuation
- Capitalization
- Clauses and Phrases
- The Sentence
- Writing Effective Sentences

Lesson 1
PARTS OF SPEECH

This is a book about the English language. You may ask, "Why do I need a book to teach me a language I already know?" True, you speak, read, and write English. You have gotten by with your present knowledge of the language, but can you move ahead with it? Is your English clear, correct, forceful, convincing? Do you fully understand everything you read or hear? Are you improving steadily in your mastery of English, accomplishing more in less time and increasing your chances for success in school or at work?

If you cannot answer all these questions with a resounding yes, this book can help you.

Let us begin with the basic elements, the blocks out of which the fabulous structure of the English language is built. Dictionary makers differ on the exact number of words in English. Some say it is a half-million; others count a million. But whatever the number, everyone agrees that all English words can be classified into eight categories called *parts of speech*. These are nouns, pronouns, verbs, adjectives, adverbs, prepositions, conjunctions, and interjections.

NOUNS

Consider nouns first. Nouns are words that name people, animals, places, things, qualities, or ideas.

People: woman, students, dentist, teenagers, Montezuma, Aunt Agatha
Animals: cat, dinosaurs, whale, peacock
Places: city, country, valley, oceans, Hoboken, Amazon River
Things: cloud, plants, dish, diamond
Qualities: strength, intelligence, brevity, brittleness
Ideas: honesty, democracy, faith, success

YOUR TURN

A.   Which of the following are nouns? It may be necessary to check the context of a word to determine if it is used as a noun. The words were taken from Lesson Eleven in Part I.

violate
grades
studies
because
right
racist
evidence
years
expression
complaint
grant

court
teenage
matter
only
school's
against
awarding
ironic
teachings

B. Find the nouns in each sentence: (from Lesson Twelve)

1. If he or she goes to the state penitentiary for four years, it will cost $50,000.
2. Rev. Jesse Jackson has been calling the public's attention to the need for moral, social, educational and economic reform.
3. Tears will get you sympathy, but sweat will get you change.
4. The real reason for the success of this charismatic preacher is the potent ideas which he communicates.
5. "I'll never forget his words at our graduation," said an 18-year-old from Atlanta.

C. Write an original sentence about each of the following:

1. a person
2. an animal
3. a place
4. a thing
5. a quality
6. an idea

COMMON AND PROPER NOUNS

Once a word has been identified as a noun, it can be further classified as either a proper noun or a common noun. A proper noun names a particular person, place or thing. It is always capitalized, as in the examples that follow.

These visitors are *Englishmen.*

Abraham Lincoln was assassinated just before the *Civil War* ended.

A common noun refers to a general class of persons, places, or things, like the italicized words in the next group of sentences.

The *letter* was mailed at the *post office.*

Many *stories* describe the *bravery* of *dogs.*

The *spectators* poured onto the *field* as the final *gun* sounded.

YOUR TURN

A. For each common noun, write an equivalent proper noun; for example,

city — Los Angeles

award — Nobel Peace Prize

1. scientist
2. motion picture

3. orchestra
4. event
5. language
6. ceremony
7. theory
8. ship
9. author
10. team

B. For each proper noun, write an equivalent common noun; for example,

Guatemala — country

Charlemagne — ruler

Hercules — hero

1. Amazon
2. Jane Fonda
3. Protestant
4. The Rolling Stones
5. Colosseum
6. Chevrolet
7. Yankees
8. Newsweek
9. Ten Commandments
10. Ronald Reagan

CONCRETE AND ABSTRACT NOUNS

Nouns may also be classified as concrete or abstract. A concrete noun names something that is material or that can be seen, heard, smelled, felt, or tasted.

The *waiter* placed the *tray* on the *table*.

A *crowd* gathered at the *theatre* to see the *celebrities*.

An abstract noun names a quality or idea that can be perceived by the mind rather than the senses.

Speak the *truth*.

Her smile spread *happiness* all around her.

YOUR TURN

A. Find the concrete nouns in the following tale.

Once there was a young moth who did not believe that the proper end of all mothkind was a zish and a frizzle. He urged all moths to reject the flame in favor of life. They all agreed. But when evening came and fires were kindled, the bugs flew off on their nightly quest for cremation.
Moral: Everybody knows better. That's the problem, not the answer.

B. Which of the following nouns are abstract? Compose five sentences with abstract nouns.

1. reason
2. sensibility
3. overture
4. oxygen
5. offer
6. philosophy
7. success
8. sleep
9. masterpiece
10. nuance

COLLECTIVE NOUNS

A collective noun names a group or collection.

Our debating *team* won first prize.

If you are thinking of the collective noun as a group or unit acting together, use a singular verb:
The class *was* listening to the lecture.

If you are thinking of the members of the group acting separately, as individuals, use a plural verb:
The committee *were* in disagreement on the choice of a new leader.

YOUR TURN

A. Which of the following are collective nouns?

1. women
2. youth
3. herd
4. community
5. members
6. family
7. class
8. gathering
9. crowd
10. student body

Note: Some nouns look plural because they end in *s*, but they take a singular verb. If you are not certain about a particular noun, consult a dictionary.

Measles is a preventable disease today.

The *news is* on at 6 o'clock.

B. Select the correct verb in each of the following:

1. Civics (was, were) offered last term.
2. Mumps (is, are) a disease of childhood.
3. The lost troop (has, have) been found.
4. The crowd at the game (is, are) expecting an upset.
5. Our team (feel, feels) confident of victory.

COMPOUND NOUNS

A compound noun is made up of two or more words. Some compound nouns are written as one word, some as two words, and still others with hyphens.

viewpoint
dining room
drive-in
guidebook
home run
self-control
jazzmen
human being
walkie-talkie
peacemaker
common sense

Consult a dictionary to determine the correct form of a compound noun.

YOUR TURN

Correct the following compound nouns where necessary:

free-for-all
pay check
machine gun
merry-maker
nightfall
boarding house
corner stone
first-class
non combatant
North Pole
status quo
steel-wool
treasure-trove
trans continental
steam engine
blood pressure
corn-syrup
firstborn
non European
right-of-way

HELPFUL HINTS

You have been identifying nouns and grouping them in various categories. There are also some grammatical clues that can help you to recognize nouns.

—1.   Nouns usually follow words like *a, an, the, this, that, some, both, each, one,* and *several.*

a book
an idea
the symphony

an impression
the goodness
a function
some chance
one story
both attempts
several benefits

—2.   Nouns usually, but not always, have a plural form.

statement — statements
child — children
foundation — foundations
analysis — analyses
alumnus — alumni
foot — feet

—3.   The most important clue for a noun (or any other part of speech) is the way it is used in the sentence. A word is a noun if it answers the question what?, who?, or whom? Note that the same word can be used as different parts of speech.

Take your *time*. (noun)

Time your reading. (verb)

The *time* element is crucial. (adjective)

YOUR TURN

A.   Apply the clues for nouns to identify the nouns in the following passage:

To save on food bills, plan before you shop. Have a pad handy so you can note what supplies are running low. Inspect your storage areas. Consult the store ads. Choose foods for their nutrition rather than taste alone. Glance at the price specials advertised in store windows.

B.   Re-read Lesson Thirteen (A Family Drama). Write a paragraph of 75-100 words explaining why you would (or would not) be willing to sign a card agreeing to donate your organs after death. Underline every noun. Also, apply to each noun the correct identification from this list: common, proper, concrete, abstract, collective or compound. Note: A noun may belong to more than one category.

PRONOUNS

Pronouns are words that take the place of nouns. Without pronouns, you have to say:

Michael, father told Michael that Michael must budget Michael's allowance.

Using pronouns, you can change the awkward sentence to:

Michael, *I* told *you* that *you* must budget *your* allowance.

Take another sentence without pronouns:

Gloria felt Gloria had done Gloria's best in the competition.

Pronouns give us:

Gloria felt *she* had done *her* best in the competition.

One last example without pronouns:

The house had been renovated recently. The house was put up for sale.

By using the pronoun *which* to replace the noun *house*, you can express the same thought in one sentence.

The house, *which* had been renovated recently, was put up for sale.

Obviously, pronouns serve a useful purpose, but you must use them properly. Which pronoun is correct in the following sentences?

(Him, He) and George are good friends.

There is a two-year age difference between Denise and (she, her).

The one (who, whom, which) has the advantage in the bout is Fred.

PERSONAL PRONOUNS

The correct form of a personal pronoun depends upon *number, gender, person* and *case.*
Number refers to singular or plural. If the word you are replacing with the pronoun (called the antecedent) is singular *(Bill, date, flag, anyone)*, use the singular form of the pronoun *(he, him, she, her, it)*. If the antecedent is plural *(members, resources, countries)*, use the plural form of the pronoun *(they, them, their)*.

Gender

Gender can be masculine, feminine, or neuter. If the antecedent of the pronoun is masculine *(Tom, man)*, use the masculine form of the pronoun *(he, him, his)*. If the antecedent is feminine *(Mindy, princess)*, use the feminine form of the pronoun *(she, her, hers)*. If the antecedent is neuter (an inanimate object like *land, water, sky*), use the neuter form of the pronoun *(it, its)*. In the plural, all three genders use the same form of the pronoun. Thus, the pronouns *they, them,* and *their* can refer to two or more men, women, or things.

Person

Pronouns have different forms for the three persons. The first person refers to the speaker. The first person pronouns are *I, me, my,* and *mine* in the singular, and *we, us, our* and *ours* in the plural. The second person refers to the person spoken to. The second person pronouns are *you, your,* and *yours* in both singular and plural. The third person refers to the person or persons, thing or things spoken of. The third person pronouns are *he, him, his, she, her, hers, it, its* in the singular, and *they, them, their* and *theirs* in the plural.

Case

The case of pronouns depends upon their use in a sentence. If the pronoun is a subject or predicate nominative, use *I, you, he, she, it, we, they,* or *who.* The choice will depend on the gender, number, and person in a particular sentence. If the pronoun is an object, use *me, you, him, her, it, us, them,* and *whom.* If the pronoun shows possession, use *my, mine, your, yours, his, her, hers, its, our, ours, their, theirs,* and *whose.*

This chart may help you keep your personal pronouns straight.

Person	Nominative	Possessive	Objective
SINGULAR first	I	my, mine	me
second	you	your, yours	you
third	he, she, it	his, her, hers, its	him, her, it
PLURAL first	we	our, ours	us
second	you	your, yours	you
third	they	their, theirs	them

YOUR TURN

A. In the following sentences, identify the pronoun according to number (singular or plural), gender (masculine, feminine, or neuter), person (first, second, or third), and case (subjective, objective, possessive). Note: *Nominative* and *subjective* are used interchangeably throughout.

Example: Every morning *he* takes the Q53 bus to school.

number — singular

gender — masculine

person — third

case — subjective

1. *We* see *them* pulling into the spacious parking lots every day.
2. In *their* hands are the green vouchers *which* entitle them to a free buffet.
3. *They* stare back at me blankly.
4. Stick to *it* until *you* win.
5. *I* consider it *my* investment for a day of entertainment.

B. Write the pronoun that fits the description.

1. first person, plural, objective case
2. second person, singular, possessive case
3. third person, singular, feminine, subjective case
4. third person, singular, neuter, possessive case
5. second person, plural, subjective case
6. first person, singular, possessive case

7. third person, plural, objective case
8. third person, singular, masculine, possessive case
9. first person, plural, possessive case
10. third person, plural, objective case

C. Choose the correct form of the pronoun.

1. In New York my sister and (I, me) visited the Twin Towers.
2. Bernice sat between Derek and (I, me).
3. The coach promised (us, we) boys a reduced fare to the game.
4. Trudy and (he, him) have been selected to represent the school.
5. The letter was addressed to Paul and (I, me).

D. Fill in the blank with the correct form of a pronoun.

1. They invited (she, her) to speak to the class.
2. The one to watch for is (he, him).
3. If I were (she, her), I would try the experiment again.
4. Jane bought tickets for (he, him) and (I, me).
5. How can you tell it was (they, them) who called?

PRONOUNS IN COMPOUNDS

When a pronoun is used with a noun, drop the noun and you will find it easier to determine the correct pronoun.

The guidance counselor spoke to (we, us) students about college. Omit *students* and you would readily choose

...spoke to us (not spoke to we)

Tara said that (we, us) girls should form our own team. Omit *girls* and the choice becomes clear.

...we should form (not us should form)

Barbara and (she, her) ran to the phone. Omit *Barbara* and the sentence reads:

...she ran (not her ran)

The most credit goes to Barbara and (she, her). Omit *Barbara* and the choice is

...credit goes to her (not to she).

YOUR TURN

Choose the correct pronoun.

1. Stanford and (I, me) interviewed the principal for *The Courier*.
2. Everyone was pleased that (we, us) amateurs performed so well.
3. After thinking it over, Roberta and (she, her) apologized for their remarks.
4. Charlene pointed out it was unfair to close the discussion to (we, us) members.
5. The assignment was completed by only two people, Francis and (I, me).

PREDICATE NOMINATIVES

A pronoun can be used as a predicate nominative. A predicate nominative follows a verb to be (*is, was, could be, should have been*, etc.), means the same as the subject, and therefore is put in the same case that you would use for the subject, the nominative case.

The winner was *she*.

She, the predicate nominative, refers to the same person as the subject, *winner*.

I shudder to think it could have been *I* in that car.

The predicate nominative, *I*, follows the verb *to be (could have been)* and means the same as the subject *it*.

Exception: The objective form of the pronoun is used with an infinitive. (An infinitive is the word *to* plus a verb.)

The guard ordered *him* to halt.

Him, not *he*, is the subject of the infinitive *to halt*.

Mrs. Belson decided to give *them* a second chance.

Them, the objective form of the pronoun, is the object of the infinitive *to give*.

The police believed the criminal to be *him*.

Him is the predicate nominative after the infinitive *to be*. Like *criminal*, the subject of the infinitive, it is in the objective case.

YOUR TURN

Choose the correct pronoun.

1. It was (they, them) who saved the game with their strong defense.
2. How could it have been (she, her) at the door when she was supposed to be on the plane to Chicago?
3. Remind Bob or (she, her) to call when they hear from the doctor.
4. If I were (he, him), I would accept the offer.
5. Since Mr. Parks wants Jim and (I, me) to help with the clean up, he should drive us home.

COMPARISONS

In a comparison, when a pronoun follows the words *than* or *as*, you can determine the correct form of the pronoun by adding the omitted or understood words.

Jim is a faster runner than (he, him).

By adding the missing word *is*, you immediately realize that the sentence requires a subject of the verb *is* understood.

Jim is a faster runner than he is (*not* him is).

"This," said the father, "doesn't hurt you as much as (I, me)."

Fill in the omitted words: …as much as it hurts me (*not*…it hurts I).

YOUR TURN

Fill in the blanks with pronouns after you have added the understood words. The meaning you choose to give certain sentences will determine the pronoun used.

1. Doris calls you more than (I, me).
2. Jan is better at science than (he, him).
3. Stan caught more passes than (they, them).
4. The teacher gave Pearl a more difficult test than (we, us).
5. I have more respect for Rose than (she, her).
6. I found this chapter more interesting than (he, him).
7. Shelley is able to read as fast as (I, me).
8. Why do you listen to Penny more than (she, her)?
9. The barber cut Bill's hair shorter than (he, his).
10. The referee called more fouls on the home team than (they, them).

GERUNDS

Use the possessive case of a pronoun before a gerund. A gerund is a word formed from a verb, ending in *-ing*, and used as a noun. (For more about gerunds, see page 162.) Gerunds used as subject: *Planting* and *harvesting* keep the farmers busy. Gerunds used as object: Children love *swimming* and *camping*.

You use the possessive case with a gerund, just as you would with any other noun.

I am surprised at *his* taking so much for granted.

His, the possessive pronoun, precedes the gerund *taking*, which is the object of *at*.

Their training is responsible for the victory.

Their, the possessive pronoun, comes before the gerund *training*, which is the subject of the verb *is*.

YOUR TURN

Choose the correct pronoun.

1. Mr. Jonas was pleased with (us, our) working overtime.
2. It seems that (me, my) planning was in vain.
3. Mother insisted on (me, my) finishing the dishes before leaving.
4. Ken resented (him, his) being taken out of the game so early.
5. The final embarrassment was (them, their) calling our bluff.
6. Mrs. Toller was annoyed at (them, their) complaining about her cooking.
7. Why do you object to (me, my) speaking so frankly?
8. There is no use in (you, your) ordering so much food for so few people.
9. The sick man could not tolerate (them, their) constant arguing.
10. Nothing is worse than (him, his) shutting out all friends from his life.

RELATIVE PRONOUNS

Till now you have been dealing with personal pronouns. Another type of pronoun is the relative pronoun, which has five forms — *that, which, who, whom,* and *whose*. The word *relative* denotes that these pronouns relate or connect a clause to another word in a sentence.

Here is the book *that* I read.

This sentence is really a combination of two sentences.

Here is the book. I read the book.

In the combined sentence, the word *that* serves a double purpose. It replaces *book* as the object of *read*, and it relates or connects the statement *I read the book* to the statement *Here is the book*.

The relative pronoun *that* may refer to a noun that is singular, plural, masculine, feminine, or neuter. The pronoun *that* may act as a subject or object in its own clause.

Here are the books that I read. (*That* refers to the plural antecedent *books* and is the object of *read*.)

Choose the dress that pleases you. (*That* refers to the singular antecedent *dress* and is the subject of *pleases*.)

That can refer to people, animals, or things. The relative pronoun *which* also has only one form, but it can refer only to animals or things, not people.

The relief organization praised the *men that* volunteered to help.

The *earthquake, which* struck both Italy and Yugoslavia, caused thousands of casualties.

The *fish, which* we had caught earlier, made a delicious dinner.

A third relative pronoun, used to refer only to people, has three forms: *who, whom, whose*. When the relative pronoun is the subject of its clause, use *who*.

Wendy is the only *one who* spoke up at the meeting. (*Who* is the subject of *spoke*.)

When the relative pronoun is the object in its clause or the object of a preposition, use *whom*.

Where is the *girl whom* you met at the skating rink? (*Whom* is the object of *met*.)

The country needs *leaders whom* we can rely on. (*Whom* is the object of *on*.)

When the relative pronoun indicates possession, use *whose*.

Where is the *student whose* paper was read? (*Whose* replaces the possessive noun *student's*.)

YOUR TURN

A.   Choose the correct pronoun.

1. Phil McCoy thought his cousin Terence was a person (who, whom) he could rely on.
2. Where is the picture (that, whom) you painted?
3. Return the tools to (whoever, whomever) gave them to you. (Hint: Treat *whoever* like *who* and *whomever* like *whom.*)
4. He sought a donor (whose, who's) bone marrow would not be rejected in a transplant.
5. We must admire someone (who, whom) has contributed so generously.
6. (Who, Whom) are you saving this seat for?
7. (Who, Whom) did Terry call last night?
8. The exhibit (who, whom, that) I enjoyed most was the auto show.
9. Einstein was a man (who, whom) influenced our ideas of time and space.
10. The spacecraft photographed Saturn (who's, whose, which) rings and moons have fascinated scientists for centuries.

B.   Re-read Lesson Fourteen ("Fearful of School"). In a paragraph of 75-100 words, tell about your first day of school (or any first time experience). Include an example of each of the different types of pronouns that have been discussed in this section: personal pronouns, pronouns used as predicate nominatives, pronouns used after *than* or *as* (in comparisons), relative pronouns. Label each pronoun according to its category.

VERBS

Every sentence has a subject and a predicate. The subject is a noun or pronoun. The most important part of the predicate — sometimes the whole predicate — is the verb.

The verb shows action or state of being. In other words, it tells what the subject is doing, has done, or will do. Or, it tells what the subject is, was, or will be. In the following sentence, the word in italics is a verb.

Professor Shnidman *studied* the problem of lateness.

You *want* to feel free.

A snowflake *flew* into my watch.

There *are* many alibis for lateness.

YOUR TURN

Find the verb in the following sentences:

1. People are often late to school or work.
2. They resent authority.
3. She heard many excuses for lateness.
4. My horoscope advised me to stay in bed today.
5. I delivered my brother's newspapers this morning.

HELPING VERBS

Some verbs, like the ones in the exercise you just did, are made up of one word. Other verbs need the help of one or more additional words.

The detour *has taken* us out of our way.

You can't just say *detour taken;* you have to say *detour has taken. Has* is a helping verb that completes the main verb *taken.*

This habit *may hurt* you and those you love.

Habit hurt is not only incorrect; it also does not say what you mean. The word *may* helps to express the idea intended.
Compare:

You *save* time.

You *can save* time.

The helping verb *can* changes the meaning.

Here is a list of helping verbs that may be added to the main verb: *am, is, are, was, were, will, be, been, being, have, has, having, had, do, does, did, may, might, can, could, shall, should.*

YOUR TURN

A.   Find the complete verb (the helping verb and the main verb).

   1.   Lateness is connected to unconscious feelings about school.
   2.   You may be bored.
   3.   That could account for your tardiness.
   4.   An undesirable habit may hurt you.
   5.   The accident could have been avoided.

B.   Write your own sentences using five of the helping words in the list.

TENSES

Verbs show the time of the action by using different forms of the verb.

I *locked* the door.

I *lock* the door.

I *will lock* the door.

The time of the action is called the tense of the verb. The main tenses are:

Present: They *enjoy* their meal.

Past: They *enjoyed* the game.

124   Future: They *will enjoy* the vacation.

By adding *-ed* to *enjoy*, we formed the past tense. By adding *will* to *enjoy*, we formed the future tense. Other tenses are formed by adding other helping verbs. For example, the perfect tenses use the helping verb *to have*.

We *have enjoyed* the party. She *has enjoyed* the visit.

The *present perfect* tense is formed when you add *have* or *has* to the main verb. This tense is used to describe an action in the recent past that continues up to the present. You would say "we have enjoyed the party" only if you are still there.

Frank realized he *had made* a mistake.

You form the *past perfect* tense when you add *had* to the main verb. This tense is used for an action in the past that came before another past action. In the example, Frank *first* made the mistake, *then* he realized it.

By the time the package arrives, we *will have left*.

The *future perfect* tense adds *will have* to the main verb. This tense is used for an action that will take place in the future *before* another future action. First we will leave, and then the package will arrive.

YOUR TURN

Identify the tense of each verb as present, past, future, present perfect, past perfect, or future perfect.

1. It *takes* an hour to drive there.
2. Prof. Shnidman *has heard* some imaginative excuses for lateness.
3. If he *had* not *driven* so fast, he could have stopped in time.
4. When *will* the drought *end*?
5. My astrologer *advised* me to stay in bed until noon today.

IRREGULAR VERBS

Some of the verbs you have been dealing with — *enjoy, lock, divide* — are called *regular* verbs because they form the past tense by adding *-ed* to the present. The past participle of these verbs, the form used in the perfect tenses, is the same as the past tense. Other verbs are *irregular*. They change internally to form the past tense and past participle.

I sleep. I slept. I have slept.

The bell rings. The bell rang. The bell has rung.

It flies. It flew. It has flown.

Study the following list of common irregular verbs. Note that the first form, the present, is the same as the infinitive and is also used with *will* or *shall* to form the future.

Present	Past	Past Participle	Present	Past	Past Participle
begin	began	begun	go	went	gone
bite	bit	bitten	know	knew	known
break	broke	broken	lie	lay	lain
bring	brought	brought	laid	laid	lain
buy	bought	bought	lose	lost	lost
catch	caught	caught	rise	rose	risen
come	came	come	see	saw	seen
do	did	done	shrink	shrank	shrunk
				shrunk	shrunken
draw	drew	drawn	sing	sang	sung
drink	drank	drunk	speak	spoke	spoken
drive	drove	driven	swim	swam	swum
eat	ate	eaten	take	took	taken
fall	fell	fallen	wear	wore	worn
forget	forgot	forgotten	write	wrote	written
give	gave	given			

YOUR TURN

A. Choose the correct form.

1. He has (broke, broken) the cup.
2. They (brought, bringed) the medicine by plane.
3. She has (catched, caught) the flu.
4. Who (drawed, drew) this picture?
5. No one has (swam, swum) in the lake recently.

B. Identify the tense of the verbs.

1. began
2. has broken
3. will give
4. has lain
5. took

C. Write your own sentences using the following verbs in the tenses indicated.

1. bite — past
2. go — present perfect
3. rise — past
4. write — past perfect
5. speak — future

TRANSITIVE VERBS

Verbs may be *transitive* or *intransitive*. A transitive verb is one which has a receiver of the action. The receiver is called the direct object.

Jack hit *the ball.*

The ball is the direct object. Ask *what* or *whom* after the verb to find the receiver of the action.

Bob left the room.
└─what?─┘

The class applauded the speaker.
└───whom?───┘

YOUR TURN

Find the transitive verbs and their direct objects (receivers).

1. Turn back the calendar pages.
2. The Nazis were starving them to death.
3. He unloaded freight cars.
4. He needed more nourishing food.
5. The father saved the potato for his son.

INTRANSITIVE VERBS

An intransitive verb has no receiver of the action. There are two types of intransitive verbs. One is a complete action by itself and has no direct object (receiver of the action).

Jack *managed* somehow. The boy's world *crumbled* before him.

The other type of intransitive verb is a linking verb. Linking verbs do not indicate action. They simply link the subject to a word or words in the predicate.

Jack *was* 14 years old at the time.

Their daily food ration *will be* muddy coffee and moldy bread.

The most common linking verbs are forms of the verb *to be (is, am, are, was, were, will be, could be)*, verbs of the senses *(tastes, feels, looks, smells, sounds)*, and verbs like *seems, appears,* and *becomes*.

YOUR TURN

Tell whether the intransitive verb in each sentence is a complete verb or a linking verb. For the linking verbs, tell which word or words in the predicate are linked to the subject.

1. That is an unlikely combination.
2. His father was lucky to work indoors.
3. The potato became the most important item in his life.
4. He dreamed about it.
5. Then it seemed impossible to find more food.

ACTIVE AND PASSIVE VERBS

Verbs can also be classified as *active* or *passive*. When the subject does the action, we say the verb is active. When the action is done to the subject, we say the verb is passive.

Active: We *paid* little attention to it. (The subject, *we*, did the action, *paid*.)
He *realized* the extent of his father's sacrifice. (The subject, *he*, did the action, *realized*.)

Passive: The inmates *were assigned* to hard labor. (The subject, *inmates*, did not do the action of assigning. The action, *were assigned*, was done to the subject.) His one "luxury" *had been withdrawn*. (The action, *had been withdrawn*, was done to the subject, *luxury*.)

Note that a passive verb uses some form of the verb to be as a helping verb, and uses the past participle to complete the verb.

YOUR TURN

A. Tell whether the verb in each sentence is active or passive.

1. Richard Stoner was turned down for his high school wrestling team.
2. Every crew member was putting forth his best effort.
3. The child was frightened by the strange noises.
4. The weekend was spent shopping and touring.
5. The package was delivered the next morning.
6. The missing papers turned up in the teacher's desk.
7. The Stoners were upset over what they felt was an act of prejudice.
8. The boys brought their equipment to camp.
9. No visitors were allowed after 8 o'clock.
10. Snow was predicted for the last day of February.

B. Re-read Lesson Six ("The Baked Potato"). Write a paragraph telling of an unusual act of sacrifice or heroism. Give the tense of each of your verbs and tell if it is regular or irregular, transitive or intransitive, active or passive.

ADJECTIVES

An adjective is a word that describes a noun or pronoun. It usually answers one of these questions:

	Noun	**Adjective + Noun**
What kind?	leaders	government leaders
	parents	anxious parents
	stakes	high stakes
	breakdowns	nervous breakdowns
	ordeal	brutal ordeal
	month	each month
Which one?	country	this country
	tests	these tests
How many?	candidates	all candidates
	subjects	six subjects
	pupils	most pupils
Whose?	lives	their lives
	machine	father's machine
	future	my future

PLACING ADJECTIVES

A noun may be described by one adjective or several adjectives. The test for the adjective remains the same: Does it answer one of the questions about the noun?

special coaching courses

a squeaking, sputtering car

What kind of courses?   special courses   coaching courses
What kind of car? squeaking car   sputtering car
Both *special* and *coaching* are adjectives. Both *squeaking* and *sputtering* are adjectives.

fairly easy questions

What kind of questions? *Easy* questions. *Easy* is an adjective. Since it does not make sense to say *fairly questions*, *fairly* is not an adjective.

An adjective usually comes before the noun it modifies, but occasionally it may come after the noun, especially in a phrase.

The hikers, *hungry* and *exhausted*, finally reached their destination.

Next came the essay question, *difficult* for some but *easy* for the politically conscious students.

A predicate adjective is an adjective in the predicate part of the sentence that describes the subject. The verb before the predicate adjective is always a linking verb.

School and state exams are *important*.

The competition is *fierce*.

Many young Chinese become *frustrated*.

POSSESSIVES

A noun or pronoun that describes another noun or pronoun is also considered an adjective. A word that answers the question Whose? must be in the possessive form. A noun answering this question must have an apostrophe.

men's shop   father's machine   factories' output   pupils' scores

A pronoun answering this question must be in the possessive case.

his judgment   their rights   anyone's guess   everybody's darling

The personal pronouns *his* and *their* are already in a possessive form; they do not need an apostrophe. The indefinite pronouns *anyone* and *everybody* add *'s*.

AGREEMENT

Most adjectives do not change; they are the same whether they describe singular or plural nouns.

popular song   popular songs

But *this* and *that* do have plural forms: *these* and *those*.

this fact   these facts   that kind of story   those kinds of stories

Be careful not to say *those kind of stories* since the plural adjective *those* cannot modify the singular noun *kind*.

COMPARISONS

When an adjective is used to compare two things or ideas, the comparative form is used.

This test was easy (difficult). The second test was easier (more difficult).

When comparing three or more things or ideas, the superlative form is used.

The last test was the easiest (most difficult) of all.

Adjectives of one syllable add *-er* and *-est* to the base form:

fierce-fiercer-fiercest

tall-taller-tallest

Adjectives ending in *-y* also add *-er* and *-est* to the base form:

pretty-prettier-prettiest

fancy-fancier-fanciest

Adjectives of two or more syllables, except those ending in *-y*, add *more* or *most* to the base form:

frequent-more frequent-most frequent

optimistic-more optimistic-most optimistic

A few adjectives are irregular, and change their form entirely in comparisons:

good-better-best

many-more-most

bad-worse-worst

little-less-least

Never use both *-er* and *more* to form the comparative, or *-est* and *most* to form the superlative:

the prettiest sight (*not* the most prettiest sight)

a friendlier tone (*not* a more friendlier tone)

YOUR TURN

A. Which words in the following list are usually adjectives?

1. important
2. seniors
3. face
4. those
5. look
6. can
7. in
8. Communist
9. poor
10. jittery

B. To each of the following nouns add an adjective that answers the question in the parenthesis:

1. (What kind of?) men   mood   speech   circus   action
2. (Which one?) word   books   attempt   nouns   degrees

3. (How many?) pairs   clowns   puzzles   positions   tasks
4. (Whose?) training   conference   ideas   hearts   assistance

C. Find the adjectives and the nouns they modify in the following sentences:

1. Chinese high school seniors face critical tests each July.
2. Those who pass can look forward to high level careers as scientists or diplomats.
3. The competition is usually fierce, the stakes are unusually high.
4. Nervous breakdowns are fairly common among students who cannot take the pressure put upon them by anxious parents.
5. The tests are necessary to develop the intellectual talent for the coming decades.
6. This procedure is relatively new.
7. The fire chief said that Marian, calm and cool-headed throughout, had saved the lives of the occupants by rousing them from their sleep.
8. This spot, far from the city noises, is ideal for your jangled nerves.
9. The witness's speech, garbled and incoherent, was of little help to the defendant.
10. The reason for this policy change is anyone's guess.

D. Write the following phrases in the comparative and superlative forms:

1. deep feelings
2. clever remarks
3. probable cause

4. astounding news
5. serious error
6. urgent need
7. close call
8. loose connection
9. good sport
10. bad record

E. Write five original sentences using predicate adjectives.

F. Re-read Lesson Sixteen ("The Use of Deadly Force"). Write a paragraph explaining your view on the question of banning the possession of firearms by civilians. Be sure to include at least five adjectives. For each adjective tell what question it answers about the noun or pronoun it modifies. Also identify any predicate adjective, comparative adjective, superlative adjective and proper adjective in your paragraph.

ADVERBS

An adverb describes a verb, an adjective, or another adverb. An adverb answers the following questions about a verb:

How: Young Rattan scrutinized her hand *intently*. (Scrutinized how? *intently*)

When: He apologized *immediately*. (Apologized when? *immediately*)

Where: They brought the baby *home*. (Brought where? *home*)

To what extent: He *barely* earns a living. (Earns to what extent? *barely*)

An adverb modifying an adjective or adverb usually answers the question How? or To what degree?

A knowledge of human nature is *extremely* helpful. (How helpful? *extremely*)

He spoke *very* carefully. (How carefully? *very*)

Some adverbs that describe adjectives and adverbs are: *so, too, fairly, somewhat, almost,* and *unusually*.

COMPARISONS

Like adjectives, adverbs also come in the comparative and superlative degrees:

He worked *more carefully* than before.

She spoke *most appreciatively* of her parents.

Adverbs of one syllable add the suffix *-er* to the base form: hard-harder. Most adverbs ending in *-ly* add *more* to the base form: more devotedly.

PLACEMENT

An adverb may be placed in different positions in the sentence, usually for the purposes of style or emphasis:

> Sometimes he works alone. He sometimes works alone. He works alone sometimes.

Note that the position of the adverb can change the meaning:

> Only Jim brought cake. (Others were expected to but didn't.)

> Jim only brought cake. (Jim was expected to do more than just bring cake but didn't.)

> Jim brought only cake. (He didn't bring anything else.)

NEGATIVES

The adverbs *hardly, barely,* and *scarcely* are negative and should therefore not be used with another negative word:

> There is hardly any room for both of us in this boat.

> We barely finished the poster in time for the parade.

> You can scarcely call that paper satisfactory.

Negative words are *no, not, nothing, none, no one,* and *neither.* Neutral, or non-negative words, are *any, anything, anyone.*

ADJECTIVES AND ADVERBS

While most words ending in *-ly* are adverbs, some are adjectives:

> stately, sickly, lovely, unruly, manly, wifely

Also, many adverbs do not end in *-ly: now, then, later, soon, here, there.* Some adjectives and adverbs have the same form: *quick, fast, early, kindly.*

YOUR TURN

A. Which words in the following list can be used as adverbs?

1. soft
2. now
3. largely
4. bright
5. traveled

6. location
7. later
8. often
9. open
10. everywhere

B. In each sentence find the adverb and the word it modifies:

1. In this situation would you have acted differently?
2. Aaron's Klan activities are totally against our teachings.
3. The principal absolutely refused to issue him a diploma.
4. With the proper grade of octane, the motor starts easily and runs well.
5. His own KKK has often broken the law.

C. Write a sentence using the following adverbs in the comparative and superlative forms:

costly   poetically   happily   kindly   little

D. For each sentence add an appropriate adverb in the space indicated:

1. I _____ would be more comfortable in the shade.
2. The teacher complimented Charles for writing so _____.
3. The cat looked _____ at the bird in the cage.
4. We had _____ reached the shelter when the storm broke.
5. Jerry looked _____ at his younger brother and _____ left the room.

E. Select the correct form:

1. Susie is (younger, more younger) than her sister.
2. He walks (steadier, more steadily) now that the fracture has healed.
3. Who is the (more, most) brilliant student in the class?
4. You did (good, well) in your essay.
5. Don has been acting (strange, strangely) all day.
6. Bill is by far the (funniest, most funniest) person I know.
7. The program showed the variety and beauty of the (vast, vastly) African landscape.
8. We had (less, fewer) complaints this term than usual.
9. This money (will, won't) hardly pay for the damages.
10. The milk tastes (sour, sourly).

F. Re-read Lesson Seventeen ("He Had a Mission in the World"). Write a paragraph describing yourself as either one who prefers to mind his own business or who gets involved. Explain why you chose this viewpoint. Be sure to include five adverbs. Try to vary the position of the adverbs from sentence to sentence. For each adverb, tell what question it answers about the word it modifies.

PREPOSITIONS

A preposition is a connecting word like *in, of, near, between,* or *outside*. It is always followed by a noun or pronoun which answers the question What? or Whom?

Richard is outstanding *in* basketball. (in what? *basketball*)

The judge ruled *against* him. (against whom? *him*)

PREPOSITIONAL PHRASES

A prepositional phrase may have more than two words in it. The noun following the preposition may have adjectives as modifiers.

> He could not compete in a fierce contact sport. (in what? *sport*)

The two adjectives *fierce* and *contact* modify the noun *sport*.

The preposition may be followed by two or more nouns that answer the question What?

> It is not a matter of Richard's ability or desire.

The two nouns *ability* and *desire* answer the question What? after the preposition *of*. *Richard's* is a possessive noun or adjective modifying both nouns.

Identifying Prepositions

The way a word is used in a sentence determines whether it is a preposition or another part of speech:

> Richard never thought of himself as handicapped before this incident.

> Richard never thought of himself as handicapped before.

In the first sentence *before* is a preposition (before what? *incident*). In the second sentence *before* is an adverb answering the question When? after *thought*.

Prepositions may show these relationships:

place: above, by, near, beside, across
direction: up, off, beyond, to, toward
association: of, between, until, with, against

Prepositions may also be made up of more than one word:
apart from, because of, by means of, in place of, in addition to

YOUR TURN

A. Which of the following can be used as prepositions?

1. an
2. upon
3. forming
4. except
5. despite
6. like
7. instead of
8. since
9. regarding
10. inside

B. In each sentence find the preposition and the noun or pronoun that answers the question What? or Whom? after it:

1. He was turned down for his high school wrestling team.
2. Rather, it was the school's concern for the boy's welfare.
3. Richard is blind in one eye.
4. The officials refused to jeopardize his sight by allowing him to compete.
5. From his early years on, he had been encouraged to take part in all physical activities.

C. Write a sentence of your own using each of the following prepositions:

1. past
2. out of
3. in behalf of
4. after
5. concerning

D. Which of the following sentences has (a) a preposition of more than one word, (b) no preposition, (c) two prepositions governing one noun, (d) two adjectives between the preposition and its noun, (e) two nouns after the preposition?

1. Richard Stoner was turned down for his high school wrestling team.
2. We are going to appeal to state and federal authorities.
3. The greater risk is to Richard's normal development and mental health.
4. No one is above and beyond the law.
5. Prior to this incident, Richard had participated in many sports.

CONJUNCTIONS AND INTERJECTIONS

CONJUNCTIONS

A conjunction is a word like *and*, *but*, and *or* that joins one part of a sentence with another.

> The "White Hand" group has executed thousands of suspected thieves *and* murderers.

> Do you agree *or* disagree with their methods?

Coordinate Conjunctions

These join words or word groups of equal rank:

> The streets *and* parks must be made safe. (*And* joins two nouns.)

> He was praised by the public *but* condemned by the police. (*But* joins two verbs.)

> You must stop this behavior *or* suffer the consequences. (*Or* joins two verb phrases.)

> They feel conventional justice moves too slowly *and* ineffectively. (*And* joins two adverbs.)

Subordinate Conjunctions

These join words or word groups of unequal rank:

He became a vigilante *because* his wife was killed by some neighborhood hoodlums.

The painter was cut down by gunfire *before* he could tell his story.

The conjunctions *because* and *before* introduce subordinate clauses that do not make sense by themselves but depend on the main clause. Other subordinate conjunctions are:

after	since
although	so that
as	unless
how	when
if	while

Paired Conjunctions

Certain coordinate conjunctions come in pairs. They are called correlative conjunctions.

Both private citizens *and* the authorities were aroused.

They did not know *whether* to support *or* to ignore him.

You are *either* with us *or* against us.

Other correlative conjunctions are:

so...as
neither...nor
not only...but also

Conjunctive Adverbs

Conjunctive adverbs serve a double purpose, as conjunctions and as adverbs. Note that a semicolon is placed before and a comma after the conjunctive adverb whenever it is used between two independent clauses.

The actions of the "White Hand" were considered illegal; *nevertheless*, it had some public support.

Other conjunctive adverbs are:

accordingly	otherwise
consequently	then
furthermore	therefore
moreover	yet

YOUR TURN

A. Select the conjunctions in the following list. Tell whether they are coordinate, subordinate, correlative, or conjunctive adverbs.

1.	after	6.	whenever
2.	therefore	7.	than
3.	as long as	8.	only
4.	in order that	9.	so that
5.	among	10.	or

B. In each sentence find the conjunctions and tell what words or word groups it joins.

1. Neither Fran nor Pat wanted the job.
2. You can build your savings by earning more or doing without.
3. Terence said he was sympathetic, but his own health problems made it impossible for him to help his dying cousin.
4. You don't know how you might act if you were in his britches.
5. He exposed himself to attack in parks and on desolate streets.

C. Complete each blank with an appropriate conjunction:

1. _____ some talent is necessary, you need not be a superstar to make the team.
2. _____ Melinda loves to bake, she volunteered to supply the cake.
3. The sky looked so threatening _____ we hesitated to go.
4. Voltaire said, "I disagree with your view, _____ I will defend your right to express your opinion."
5. The best defense, _____ all good generals say, is a strong offense.

D. Use conjunctions to combine the following groups of sentences into one sentence:

1. The actor was cheered by many audiences. They were happy to see a private citizen putting the criminals on the run.
2. Two inches of rain fell in the thunderstorm. The thunderstorm toppled power lines. The thunderstorm disrupted traffic.
3. White Hand members break into the homes of known criminals. They shoot them. They then inform police where the bodies are.
4. The program calls for more military spending. The program calls for tax reductions. The program calls for budget cutbacks.
5. The head of the subway system announced a fare increase. He also said that could be followed by a further increase. The state legislature's decision to levy a new tax will make the second increase unnecessary.

INTERJECTIONS

An interjection is a word or group of words that expresses strong feeling. The interjection has little or no connection with the rest of the sentence.

Oh, I see it now.   *Nonsense!* The accusation is a complete lie.

A mild interjection is followed by a comma. A strong interjection is followed by an exclamation mark. Some interjections are:

pst   my goodness   hey   well   alas   oh   dear   ouch   wow   hurrah   ugh

YOUR TURN

A. List three words or phrases that can be used to show the following:

1. surprise   2. disappointment   3. pleasure   4. pain   5. admiration

B. Write a sentence using each of the following interjections:

1. ah   2. my word   3. golly   4. pft   5. fiddlesticks

C. Re-read Lesson Eighteen ("A Mother's Decision"). Write a paragraph telling why you agree or disagree with Mrs. D'Aversa's decision. Consider this question: Do you apply the same standards to strangers as you do to family members? For each preposition in your paragraph, name its object. For each conjunction, tell whether it is coordinate or subordinate, a correlative conjunction or a conjunctive adverb.

Lesson 2
PUNCTUATION

Punctuation marks serve as signals to make the meaning clear. Without punctuation marks the following sentence could have two possible meanings:

Alan said the teacher is late again.

This could be punctuated to mean that the teacher is late.
Alan said, "The teacher is late again."

Or it could be punctuated to mean that Alan is late again.
"Alan," said the teacher, "is late again."

Punctuation marks also help to avoid confusion:
After eating Howard felt too full to go swimming.

You might have to read this sentence twice before realizing that a pause is necessary between *eating* and *Howard*.
After eating, Howard felt too full to go swimming.

END PUNCTUATION

The punctuation marks that end a sentence are the period, the question mark, and the exclamation mark.

PERIODS

The period is used at the end of a statement or a mild command:

The subway fare has been increased again.

Please pass your papers forward.

Periods are also used after abbreviations of places, titles, degrees, and time expressions:

U.S.A.   Washington, D.C.   Jan.   Mrs. Fenton   Martin Luther King, Jr.

10 P.M.   2:30 A.M.   576 B.C.

(but UFO   HUD   FBI   CARE)

Initials in names are also followed by periods:

P.T. Barnum   H.L. Mencken   T.S. Eliot

QUESTION MARKS

The question mark is used after a question:

Does it matter? Why did you leave so early?

In a direct quotation put the question mark after the complete question:

"Why did you quit?" he asked.

"Why," he asked, "did you quit?"

No question mark is needed in an indirect question, that is, when the exact words of the questioner are not used:

He asked her why she quit. (The words *why she quit* are not the exact words of the speaker.)

EXCLAMATION MARKS

The exclamation mark is used after a strong statement that expresses surprise, shock, or some other powerful emotion:

Get ready! Ten seconds to touchdown!

Impossible! He wouldn't lie to me!

"What a prize!" Terry beamed.

YOUR TURN

Insert the missing punctuation marks:
1. Rev Mills will speak at 3:30 P M
2. Run for your lives The building is collapsing
3. Splendid We'll announce the results on the 6P M news
4. Have you heard that Mrs Burns has moved to St Croix
5. Franklin K Lorenz met his future wife, Patricia L Kronn, when they were both in the Ph D program at Princeton
6. Don't keep us in suspense Is it a boy or a girl
7. Expensive I should say they were
8. "Do you think," he asked, "the baseball strike will soon be over"
9. He asked if I thought the baseball strike would soon be over
10. Detective O J Flanagan examined the fragments of the broken ashtray and his face lit up with a knowing smile

THE COMMA

A comma indicates a brief pause.

SERIES

Commas are used between the parts of a series: (A series must have three or more words, phrases, clauses, or numbers.)

The Constitution guarantees us the right to life, liberty, and the pursuit of happiness.

The Gettysburg Address ends with the stirring words "that government of the people, by the people, and for the people shall not perish from the earth."

The teacher announced the test would be based on chapters 3, 4, 5, and 6.

Do not use a comma if all parts of a series are joined by *and, or,* or *nor.*

I concede that your argument is clear and strong and irrefutable.

An accident can result from ignorance or negligence or stubbornness.

INTRODUCTORY EXPRESSIONS

Introductory words such as *well, why, oh, yes,* and *no* are followed by a comma.

Oh no, I wouldn't dream of it.

Well, that settles it.

MODIFIERS

Introductory Modifiers

A comma is used after a participial phrase, a dependent clause, or a long prepositional phrase at the beginning of a sentence:

Heeding his master's voice, the horse plunged forward. (participial phrase)

When the cat's away, the mice will play. (adverbial clause)

In a situation like this, try to remain calm. (2 prepositional phrases)

Nonessential Modifiers

A nonrestrictive expression, that is, words that add nonessential information, is set off with commas before and after:

Betty, looking very pleased with herself, won first prize in the essay contest.

Cantaloupe, available in the market now, is a source of vitamin C.

Bess Claridge, who was recently married, was my neighbor for ten years.

The girl who was recently married to Elmer Cole was my neighbor for ten years.

In the first three sentences above, the expressions set off by commas can be removed from the sentence without changing the basic meaning of the sentence. In the last sentence, however, the clause *who was recently married to Elmer Cole* is necessary to identify the girl; therefore, no commas are used to set off this restrictive clause.

Appositives

Commas set off appositives (an appositive is a noun placed next to another noun to explain or identify it) that adds nonessential information:

> We boarded the plane, a 747, for the trip to Hawaii.

> The two finalists, Marian and Eleanor, were very evenly matched.

When the appositive adds essential information or is needed to identify the noun, the commas are omitted.
> My friend Kim owns a moped.

> The figure 8 is difficult to execute for a beginning skater.

DIRECT ADDRESS

A noun of direct address, that is, the name of the person the speaker is talking to, is always set off with commas.

> Frankly, Coach Benson, I feel I have warmed the bench long enough.

> Of course, Laura, this is strictly between us.

INTERRUPTIONS

Commas set off parenthetical or transitional phrases like *on the other hand* and *as you know*:

> On the other hand, you may never find a bargain like this again.

> The train, I think, has arrived.

COMPOUND SENTENCE

When a conjunction joins two main clauses, a comma is used before the conjunction.

> Pearl called several times, but all she got was a busy signal.

> The serum has been fully tested, and it has lived up to our expectations.

ADJECTIVES

Commas are used to separate coordinate adjectives (adjectives are coordinate if the word *and* can replace the comma between them) that modify the same noun:

> This is a risky, untested venture.

The word *and* can replace the comma between *risky* and *untested*.

> Dr. Barnes owns an expensive red sports car.

The three adjectives are not coordinate; they cannot be separated by *and*.

DATES AND ADDRESSES

Commas are used between the parts of an address and of a date:

> The Weilers have lived at 2204 Gretchen Street, Milwaukee, Wisconsin since June 11, 1981.

OMISSIONS

Commas can indicate that words have been omitted:

> Lot chose the Jordan Valley; Abraham, the hills.

> Kenny mentioned the incident frequently; Tom, never.

CLARITY

> Outside, the helicopter hovered over the tragic scene.

> After all, the letters were addressed to me, not to you.

REMEMBER:

Do not use a comma:

—1. between a subject and predicate

Several new buildings(,) will be added to the campus.

—2. between a verb and its complement

Florence called(,) her mother in the evening.

—3. before an indirect quotation

Helen replied(,) that she had no intention of making coffee for her boss.

—4. before the first item or after the last item of a series

Will you have(,) cake, pie, or pudding(,) for dessert?

—5. between two main clauses not joined by a conjunction

Helen decided to appeal the case. The judge ruled in her favor.

(A semicolon, but not a comma, may be used instead of the period.)

—**6.**   to set off restrictive phrases, clauses, or appositives

> A boss(,) who has a low boiling point(,) will not keep his employees for long.

(The statement is restricted only to a boss *who has a low boiling point.*)

—**7.**   if the meaning is clear without it

> The officials at the unemployment office ruled that Helen had left her job voluntarily and was not entitled to receive unemployment compensation.

YOUR TURN

A.   Give the reason for each comma in the following sentences:

1. They offer a variety of useful courses and, ultimately, a degree.
2. There are a few colleges, however, that operate in a shady manner.
3. One of the most notorious was Pacific College in Los Angeles, California.
4. To illustrate how easy it was to get an advanced degree from such diploma mills, Assemblyman Stavisky enrolled his German shepherd, Shanna, at Pacific College.
5. He received a letter that read, "Welcome, my friend, to Pacific College."

B.   Insert commas where needed in the following sentences, and explain why.

1. For all the reasons that have been mentioned we should choose our college carefully.
2. Well since you put it that way I accept your apology.
3. Sam reached into his pocket drew out a five-dollar bill and handed it to Margie his niece.
4. You can take all the time you need but you must not take wild guesses.
5. Talcum powder works like a charm in repelling flea beatles on tomatoes potatoes peppers and other plants.
6. Well-hidden from view amidst bouquets of long-stemmed multi-colored roses the camera recorded every moment of the scene.
7. On June 6 1944 D-Day the Allies launched the attack across the Channel.
8. Yes I checked Ronald's address. It is 225 West Harbor Road El Paso Texas.
9. After a pause of several minutes Joan as you might have guessed selected a blue dress; Anna a green one.
10. Above the sky was blue. Unfortunately before the day ended the clouds began to gather and the trip home which should have taken one hour dragged out into several hours of detours traffic jams and frustration.
11. "Okay lady" the driver asked "where to?"

C.   Write five original sentences using commas for at least five different reasons.

SEMICOLON AND COLON

SEMICOLONS

A semicolon indicates a stronger pause than a comma and a weaker pause than a period. It cannot end a sentence.

Compound Sentences

A semicolon separates the two main clauses of a compound sentence when they are not joined by

a coordinate conjunction *(and, but, or).*

Be careful about selecting a name for a child; it could affect his or her development.

Sticks and stones may break our bones; names can harm us too.

A semicolon is used between the clauses of a compound sentence joined by conjunctive adverbs like *consequently, furthermore,* and *however.*

The Census Bureau reports that the most popular name for American boys was John; however, it has now been replaced by Michael, Jason, and David.

Other conjunctive adverbs are:

as a result
besides
for example
for instance
hence
in addition
in fact
meanwhile
moreover
namely
otherwise
similarly
indeed
then
thus

Use a semicolon before the coordinating conjunction of a compound sentence if either clause already has two commas in it or if the sentence is overly long:

Do not pick a name which can be used by either sex such as Lee, Robin, or Leslie; nor should you choose a dated name.

SERIES

When any of the parts of a series already contain commas, use semicolons to divide the series clearly:

The article on names tells us that popular names for girls are Jennifer, Amy, Sarah, and Michelle; that parents should not give a child a name like Arthur Seymour Sullivan because of the problem created by the initials; and that a child should not be named after a father because he has a right to his individuality.

The examinations will be given on Monday, May 14; Tuesday, May 15; and Thursday, May 17.

YOUR TURN

A. Add a semicolon in the appropriate place in the following sentences:

1. The game is over the athletes retreat to their locker rooms to shower and change. **145**

2. Newspapermen have always used that time for interviews however women reporters were barred from the locker room.
3. The judge left the arrangements up to the club management. He suggested allowing a short time period for all interviews before players removed their uniforms or, if the club wished, barring the locker room to all of the media.
4. Melissa Lincoln is a talented, level-headed, no-nonsense reporter she resents the unfair advantage her male colleagues have over her in covering a sports event.
5. Ms. Lincoln said, "Women reporters are not just looking to get publicity they want a chance to compete on an equal level with men."

B. Compose three sentences, each one illustrating a different use of the semicolon.

COLONS

Introductions

The colon is used:

—1. to introduce a list:

Great riches wait for the person who can do any of the following: invent stockings that never run, find a plentiful substitute for gasoline, or discover a cure for baldness.

—2. to introduce an explanation:

Only one question remained: Will it work?

—3. before a long quotation or after a formal introduction:

Thomas Jefferson wrote: "We hold these truths to be self-evident..."

Conventions

The colon is also used:

—4. after the salutation in a business letter:

Dear Sir: Gentlemen: My dear Mrs. Perkins:

—5. between hours and minutes in expressing time:

2:15 P.M.   8:57 A.M.

YOUR TURN

Add the colon where necessary and give the rule that applies:
1. The nominee declined the award with these words "I cannot accept this honor when more deserving candidates have been passed over."
2. Contestants were judged in the following categories short stories, poems, essays, and speeches.

3. Celia's running mates included the following Phil, vice-president; Alice, treasurer; and Vince, secretary.
4. At 7 30 P.M. I started Chapter 1. A half-hour later I was still at the same point; the reason an "important" telephone call.

5. The Food and Drug Administration tested the long-range effect of these substances sweeteners, additives, and preservatives.

DASH AND HYPHEN

DASHES

The dash is used:

—1. to indicate a sudden break or shift in thought:

Here is my opinion — but no, let's leave it for another time.

—2. to set off a sudden parenthetical expression added almost as an afterthought:

Max knows — he is my brother, after all — that I would vouch for his honesty.

—3. to summarize a thought or to introduce a thought you wish to emphasize:

The shimmering lake, the lofty mountains, the quiet woods — all had a calming effect on Mr. Pinkerton.

You leave me only one recourse — to sue.

—4. to indicate that a word is incomplete:

Captain L — Mrs. R —

—5. to set off a long or punctuated appositive:

I visited my cousins — Beatrice, Alice, and Kitty — during the vacation.

YOUR TURN

A. Punctuate with dashes where necessary and give the reason:

1. You'll be surprised I know I was to hear who won the debate.
2. The first day of each new school year brings with it great excitement, anticipation, goose bumps and some tears.
3. When Mrs. K gives an assignment, you'd better have it ready the next day.
4. The traumatic experience of being in a closet on her first day of school left a deep scar on the child for years to come.

B. Compose three sentences, each one illustrating a different use of the dash.

HYPHENS

The hyphen (shorter than the dash) is used:

—1. in many compound words

senator-elect   self-esteem   court-martial   brother-in-law

commander-in-chief   half-baked   ex-president   U-turn

—2. between two words that act as a single adjective before a noun:

a sure-footed pony   a level-headed young man

—3. in compound numerals from twenty-one to ninety-nine:

eighty-six

—4. to divide a word between syllables at the end of a line:
These words can be divided at any point where there is a hyphen.

hur-ri-cane   in-ter-cep-tor   mac-ad-am   pa-ren-the-sis   ques-tion-a-ble

Do not hyphenate words of one syllable or even two-syllable words with fewer than five letters.
Do not divide a one-letter syllable from the rest of the word (a-round, milk-y).

YOUR TURN

A. Place the hyphens where necessary:

1. stepping stones to success
2. head to head confrontation
3. seventy six trombones
4. second hand information
5. second class citizen
6. a see saw battle
7. a second story man
8. eighty two
9. twenty five
10. clear blue sky

B. Decide which of these words could be divided at the end of a line, and show where the divisions could come:

1. responsibility
2. prefabricate
3. far fetched
4. dictatorial
5. corpse
6. buttermilk
7. area
8. extremity
9. junior
10. meandering

148   C. Compose three sentences to illustrate different uses of the hyphen.

PARENTHESES AND BRACKETS

PARENTHESES

Parentheses are used:

—1.   to enclose extra or incidental comments that a speaker adds to a sentence.
The material is often not part of the main statement and is not grammatically connected with it:

> The records (We bought them when they were on sale last week) proved to be the hit of the party.

—2.   to enclose letters or numbers in a list:

> The mayor ticked off the major problems facing the city: (1) crime, (2) poverty, (3) unemployment (4) pollution, and (5) congestion.

—3.   to enclose dates after the name of a historic figure:

> We have been studying the political theories of John Locke (1632–1704).

Explanations or additional words can be set off by commas, dashes, or parentheses Use commas for material close to the main thought of the sentence, dashes for material that is not so close, and parentheses for material that is so loosely related that it might be made a separate sentence.

YOUR TURN

A.   Add parentheses where necessary and give your reason:

1.   Just when the party was about to fizzle out would you believe it? the entertainers arrived.
2.   Riza Khan Pahlavi 1877-1944 was the Shah of Persia.
3.   When Dad came and none too soon, as it turned out the argument was getting out of hand.
4.   James Langston Hughes 1902-1967 was a famous poet and writer who popularized the character Simple.
5.   The fox how deceptive a creature can be commenced to compliment the crow on its beautiful voice.

BRACKETS

Brackets are used to set off material the writer adds to identify or explain something in a quotation:

> The general announced: "On this historic day [July 20], we have begun the counterattack that will send the invader from our land."

YOUR TURN

A.   Add brackets where necessary: (Assume in each case the writer is adding the name.)

1.   The jury foreman declared, "We find the defendant Albert Larkin not guilty."
2.   The note read: "Do not worry. The boy Eric is safe and we are bringing him home."
3.   On the envelope was the name Ricard Richard.

B.   Compose three sentences using parentheses and brackets correctly.

APOSTROPHES

OMISSIONS

The apostrophe is used to show that letters have been omitted to form a contraction. The apostrophe is placed where the letter is omitted.

does not = doesn't   he will = he'll   she had or she would = she'd   it is = it's

Note: Do not use an apostrophe in the possessive form of personal pronouns: ours, yours, his, hers, its, theirs.

Apostrophes also indicate missing numbers:

an '81 graduate   the '79 World Series

POSSESSION

—1.   To form the possessive of singular nouns, add an apostrophe and an *s*:

Sarah's friend   the door's hinges   the cat's paw   an hour's delay

—2.   for plural nouns ending in *s*, add only an apostrophe:

ladies' coats   ten dollars' worth   students' cafeteria   teachers' conference

—3.   for plural nouns not ending in *s*, add an apostrophe and an *s*:

the children's hour   the men's share   the editors-in-chief's   resignations

Note: In a compound expression, the apostrophe belongs with the part nearest the object possessed:

Sid's and Carrie's reports (each gave a separate report)

Sid and Carrie's reports (both worked together on the reports)

YOUR TURN

A.   Place the apostrophe where necessary and give the rule that applies:

1.   Dr. Sheffs staff treats the whole family together because they know that a childs anxiety often stems from parental tensions.
2.   Havent you prepared the childrens room yet?
3.   Its not yesterdays failure Im concerned with but tomorrows possibilities.
4.   The two cars trunks flew open.
5.   Its obvious that the cat likes to take its time.

B.   Compose three sentences to illustrate different uses of the apostrophe.

QUOTATION MARKS

Quotation marks are used to enclose someone's exact words, spoken or written:

"We had no idea it was a 12-year-old boy," the red-faced tax agents said.

"If we had known," they added, "it would have been handled differently."

Quotation marks are also used around the titles of short pieces of writing such as poems, songs, short stories, articles, and chapters that are part of longer works.

The story I enjoyed most in *The O. Henry Reader* was "The Third Ingredient."

For the Regents examination you should prepare yourself with a few essays like Emerson's "Self-Reliance" and several poems like Shelley's "Ozymandias."

Note: Use single quotation marks to enclose a quotation within a quotation:
Jody's mother asked the agents, "Did you say to Jody, 'We will take punitive action against you'?"

PUNCTUATE DIALOGUE

Place commas and periods inside quotation marks, semicolons and colons outside quotation marks, and quotation marks or exclamation points inside or out depending on whether the direct quotation or the entire sentence is the question or exclamation:

Did you say, "Jan has the tickets"? (The whole sentence is a question.)

She asked, "Does Jan have the tickets?" (The direct quotation is a question.)

"Does Jan have the tickets?" she asked. (The direct quotation is a question.)

YOUR TURN

A. Add quotation marks to the following sentences and give the rules that apply:

1. The proof of the pudding, said the wise man, smacking his lips, is in the eating.
2. When asked what impelled her to jump from the burning building, Melanie replied, I remembered the proverb He who hesitates is lost.
3. Fair ball, called the umpire, but the crowd roared Foul!
4. I know how awful it must be for you, Henry, his mother pleaded, but you must go to school. After all, you are the principal.
5. Whitman's poem O Captain! My Captain! is as well-known as Melville's novel Moby Dick.

B. Compose three sentences that illustrate the correct use of quotation marks.

ITALICS

Italics in print use a type that slants the letters right. In longhand or typewriting, indicate italics by underlining.

Use italics for the titles of long, complete works (books, full-length plays, films, magazines, newspapers) and for the names of ships, trains, or planes:

> For tomorrow read the Prologue to *The Canterbury Tales.*

> While traveling on the *Queen Elizabeth II*, Mr. Florio read *The New York Times* and *National Geographic.*

Italics are also used

—1. for foreign words:

> *nouveau riche   status quo   ibid.*

—2. for words, letters, and figures referred to as such:

> He was eliminated from the spelling bee because he did not know that the word *rotisserie* had two *s*'s.

—3. for words that are emphasized:

> You must *always* wear protective goggles when you use an electric sander.

YOUR TURN

A. Underline the words that should be in italics:

1. The program included Rachmaninoff's Prelude in C-Sharp Minor and excerpts from Bizet's Carmen.
2. Both Time and Newsweek contained lengthy features on the Ottawa Conference.
3. Leonard earned his B.A. degree magna cum laude.
4. To form the plural of city, drop the y and add ies.
5. "A true gourmet," Clyde emphasized, "would never never drown his food in ketchup."

B. Compose three sentences to illustrate different uses of italics.

Lesson 3
CAPITALIZATION

The rules for capitalization vary from one language to the next. Some languages never use capital letters. Others capitalize all nouns. English takes the middle road. We capitalize two main classes of nouns.

BEGINNINGS

The first word of every sentence is always capitalized:

> *K*eep trying. *Y*our talent and experience are going to be recognized.

The first word of a direct quotation is capitalized *only* when the quotation is a complete sentence:

> The judge said, "*E*ach individual's rights must be respected."

> He ruled that there is no duty "*t*o save someone's life."

The first word of a line of poetry is usually capitalized:

> *C*onsider the auk,
> *B*ecoming extinct because he forgot how to fly and could only walk.

NAMES

All proper nouns, that is, words that name a specific person, place, thing, or idea, are capitalized. This includes names of:

—1. people

   Barry   Melissa

—2. places

   Central Park   Jones Beach   Mount Rushmore

—3. religions, the Bible, and God

   Judaism   Genesis   the Lord

—4. buildings

Twin Towers   Taj Mahal

—5. organizations and institutions and their abbreviations

the Rand Corporation   Harvard University   United Nations   N.O.W.

—6. historical events

the War of Roses   the Camp David Agreement

—7. holidays

Thanksgiving   Passover   Halloween

—8. ships, trains, and planes

Old Ironsides   Amtrak Concorde

—9. titles used with the names of people

Captain Newman   Aunt Ellen   Senator Jackson

—10. common nouns when they are part of a proper noun

Hudson River   House Rules Committee   Mark Twain Junior High School

—11. the words *I* and *O*, and words like *Mother, Father, Sis, Son* when these are used in place of a person's name:

As much as I love you, *Mom*, it's time for me to leave and go out on my own.

—12. every important word in titles
This includes titles of books, plays, magazines, and newspapers. The only words you do not capitalize in titles are prepositions, conjunctions, and articles that have fewer than five letters and are not the first or last word of the title:

The Winter of Our Discontent
Stars to Steer By
There's Too Much Scare Talk About Cancer
When Lilacs Last in the Dooryard Bloomed

—13. the words *North, South, East,* and *West* and such words as *Northeast* when they refer to a particular section of the world or of a country:

Go *south* for six blocks, then *east*. (direction)

Lewis and Clark opened a new trail to the West. (section)

—14.   school subjects that are languages or that are the name of a particular course, not just a subject area:

French
chemistry
Latin
Physics 2
Spanish
American history
English
Bookkeeping 1

—15.   the days of the week and months of the year but not the seasons

The first Monday in September signals the end of summer.

—16.   adjectives formed from proper nouns

Danish pastry
French cuisine
Southern hospitality
Haitian painters

YOUR TURN

A. Which of the following are capitalized?

1. uncle ted
2. fourth of july
3. gymnastics
4. the battle of waterloo
5. america the beautiful
6. spca
7. romeo and juliet
8. the west wind
9. japanese imports
10. australian bush

B. Rewrite the following sentences, using capital letters when necessary. State the rule that applies in each case.

1. caroline received an acceptance from st. paul's junior college in the fall.
2. how long can the teamsters union hold out against the western electric company?
3. the shakespearean play i have been reading, *the taming of the shrew*, has been modernized for broadway as the musical *kiss me, kate.*
4. last week stan and i saw a baseball game between the new york yankees and the boston redsox.
5. "is there any reason," mr. myers asked, "why this law should not apply to men and women equally?"

C. Write original sentences in which the following words are correct as written:

1. doctor
2. Father
3. southeast
4. General
5. avenue
6. Corporation
7. Secretary
8. Chief
9. Road
10. university

Lesson 4
CLAUSES AND PHRASES

CLAUSES

A clause is a group of words containing a subject and predicate. If the clause expresses a complete thought without requiring further explanation, it is a sentence.

The algebra teacher is lazy.

Professor Oak places the blame for cheating on the teacher's shoulders.

If a word like *who, that, since* or *although* introduces the clause, it can no longer stand alone as a sentence. Something must be added to complete the thought. Such a clause is called a dependent or subordinate clause.

As the teacher turns his back

The sentence is not complete until you tell what happens as the teacher turns his back.

As the teacher turns his back, you have a minute to look at a classmate's paper.

...which her second period students took

The sentence is not complete until you tell what the students took.

She gives your fifth period class the same test which her second period students took.

There are three kinds of dependent clauses:

—1. an adjective clause

Over 2000 readers responded to a column *which Ellis Sloane writes.*

The adjective clause describes the noun *column.* (which column?)

—2. an adverbial clause

An assistant is proctoring *while the regular teacher is in the library.* The adverbial clause describes the verb *is proctoring.* (tells when)

—3. a noun clause

Several students said *that their parents had set poor examples for them.*

The noun clause is a direct object (said what?)

YOUR TURN

A. Identify the following as complete sentences, subordinate clauses, or phrases:

1. The Englishwoman who named her twins Peter and Repeater.
2. In one of the greatest films of the century.
3. The Fools' weird judgment in selecting the name Ima for their daughter.
4. Names have much to do with how a person learns to cope in the world.
5. These remedies have been tested over the years.
6. To protect ripening tomatoes from fungal diseases.
7. Unless you provide all the necessary parts.
8. It is up to us to create our own opportunities.
9. Because their parents saddled them with inappropriate names.
10. Before the drugs destroy our generation.

B. Identify the italicized word groups as adjective clauses, adverbial clauses, or noun clauses: (Some sentences have more than one dependent clause.)

1. Remember *that it's always better to be wise than to be smart.*
2. Life is meaningless *unless you bring meaning to it.*
3. *When the challenge comes,* will you be ready?
4. Children are being born now *who won't have the same rights (that) you do unless you act.*
5. I see that crinkle on your brow *that signals your doubt.*
6. *What you'll discover* will be wonderful.
7. Those are my parting words *as you face the future.*
8. Prof. Ashley offers good advice to parents *who are getting ready to name their new babies.*
9. *Since every child has a right to his individuality,* he should not be named after his father.
10. Prof. Ashley thinks *that parents should be very careful when picking names for their children.*

C. Complete each sentence with the subordinate clause indicated in the blank. The introductory word of the clause has been supplied.

1. I am frequently struck by the fact that (noun clause).
2. Do not worry about what (noun clause).
3. Your problem won't disappear simply because (adverbial clause).
4. I felt so relieved it felt as though (adverbial clause).
5. For one who (adjective clause), this is not an easy task.

REMEMBER:

A dependent clause must satisfy three conditions:
1. It must have a subject and verb (apart from those in the main clause).
2. It must have an introductory word (this word can be understood).
3. It cannot express a complete thought by itself.

ADJECTIVE CLAUSES

Adjective clauses are introduced by the pronouns *which, that, who, whose,* or *whom.* These pronouns have a triple job. They introduce the adjective clause; they refer to a word in the main clause (the antecedent); and they serve as subject, object, or possessive pronoun within the adjective clause. **157**

This is the part *that* I remember best.

That introduces the adjective clause; it is a pronoun referring to the antecedent *part*; and it is the direct object of the verb *remember* in the adjective clause.

The choir leader called on Barry, *who* sang several songs.

Who introduces the adjective clause; it is a pronoun referring to the antecedent *Barry*; and it is the subject of the verb *sang* in the adjective clause.
Some sentences omit the introductory word *that*.

Here is the present (that) I promised you.

That is understood. Its antecedent is *present*. It is the direct object of the verb *promised*.

YOUR TURN

The introductory word of the adjective clause is italicized. Give its antecedent in the main clause and tell whether it is a subject or object in the adjective clause.
1. He entered into a partnership with David *which* proved very profitable.
2. Laughter actually improves the health of those *who* suffer certain illnesses.
3. This is the type of behavior *that* seems unmanageable.
4. The teacher returned all the papers *that* she had marked.
5. Fleeing from the avalanche *that* threatened their lives, the rescuers stumbled on the survivors.
6. There was an envelope protruding from Jerry's jacket, *which* hung behind the door.
7. When Mrs. D'Aversa called, Rev. Tallman signalled to the detective with *whom* he had been talking.
8. As she tiptoed to the room, she heard voices *that* she recognized as those of her son and his friend.
9. Jerry and Dom were counting a huge stack of bills, *which* they had apparently stolen from the church.
10. Mrs. D'Aversa was a widow *who* had done her best to raise her children to be God-fearing.

ADVERBIAL CLAUSES

An adverbial clause can describe a verb, an adjective, or an adverb in the main clause.

The bell rang *before I could finish the exam.*

The adverbial clause modifies the verb *rang.*
The test was harder *than I had expected.*

The adverbial clause modifies the adjective *harder.*
George was so nervous *that he could not do his best.*

The adverbial clause modifies the adverb *so.*

Conjunctions

Learn to recognize the subordinate conjunctions that signal the beginning of an adverbial clause. Some examples are:

after
although
as if
because
if
so that

than
until
when
where
while
unless

Omissions

The adverbial clause introduced by *than* and *as* may have some parts understood.

> Robin was better prepared for the exam *than* I (was).
> Fred felt as tense after the exam as (he felt) before.

YOUR TURN

A. Identify the adverbial clause and tell what verb, adjective, or adverb in the main clause it modifies:

1. Are no-calorie cola drinks on your menu because you are trying to lose weight?
2. The patient was so determined to recover that the doctors themselves were impressed.
3. If foods and beverages won't get us, we can expect to be finished off by the poisoned atmosphere and acid rain.
4. Since the party was almost over, Robert felt it was not improper to leave.
5. When the alarm sounded in the middle of the night, Claire ran to the children.
6. The cast ran through a complete dress rehearsal so that they would be completely prepared.
7. The mountainous waves tossed the liner about as if it were a toy boat.
8. Stephen would not leave his sister until the doctor had assured him she was out of danger.
9. Nero fiddled while Rome burned.
10. The health faddists are so alarmist that they even suspect mother's milk of being troublesome.

B. Fill in the understood parts of the adverbial clauses.

1. While _____ driving, Jim noticed a vacancy sign at a motel.
2. Juanita is more attracted to Tom than _____ to Phil.
3. Juanita is more attracted to Tom than Henrietta _____.
4. Though he has had less training, Jerry plays as well as Ronald _____.
5. The report, though _____ brief, has all the essential points.

C. Combine each pair of sentences by making an adverbial clause out of one sentence. To introduce the adverbial clause, choose a subordinate conjunction that expresses the proper relationship between the two sentences.

1. He was disappointed. He was not chosen for the team.
2. Wanda hurried. She did not arrive until after the speech had begun.
3. Call me this evening. You may need my help with the homework.
4. Most people don't live within their income. They don't consider that living.
5. Improvements protect the value of your home. Costs continue to rise.
6. The mind was willing. The body was not.
7. She waited on the platform. The train came.
8. The fight spilled over into the street. The crowd joined in.
9. Senator Shelton made a strong speech in favor of the bill. The Senate passed it overwhelmingly.
10. Mr. Clark made a promise to support us. I doubt that he will.

NOUN CLAUSES

A noun clause acts in a sentence exactly like a noun.

Noun as subject: The *accusation* stunned Perry.

Noun clause as subject: *That he should be accused of dishonesty* stunned Perry.

Noun as direct object: The proctor announced the *time*.

Noun clause as direct object: The proctor announced *that the test would end at noon*.

Noun as predicate nominative: The question was *why*.

Noun clause as predicate nominative: The question was *why he had not voted*.

Noun as appositive: Earl's request, a *plea* for a postponement, was refused.

Noun clause as appositive: Earl's request, *that the test should be postponed*, was refused.

Noun as object of a preposition: They spoke about the *difficulty* of the exam.

Noun clause as object of a preposition: They spoke about *how difficult the exam was*.

The noun clause, like the adjective and adverbial clause, may sometimes omit the introductory word:

Most students felt (that) they had passed.

YOUR TURN

A. Identify the noun clause and tell how it is used in the sentence (subject, object, predicate noun, appositive, object of a preposition):

1. What you have learned is the truth.
2. The reason for the delay in the game is that some of our players were late.
3. Corinne and her companions spoke of what they had learned from the experience.
4. Following the adage that there is no place like home, Penny decided to attend a local college.
5. Too late we discovered that the road had been washed out.
6. Edward saw that a man was dragging a nurse into a van at knife point.
7. The fact that his own life was in danger did not deter him.
8. It is fair to say that his reaction was instinctive.
9. I think I will always feel guilty about that.
10. There is no doubt that he fulfilled his mission in the world.

B. Combine the following pairs of sentences by using a noun clause.

1. Parents have a sincere hope. They want their children to be happy and successful.
2. Mark is very well-informed. This was easily proved in his speech.
3. I heard the good news. Our candidate had won.
4. The young palm reader explained to the reporter. He had noticed a lighter skin tone on the woman's ring finger.
5. Sandra may get the job. It depends on her interview.

C. Compose original sentences using two examples of each: adjective clause, adverbial clause, noun clause.

PHRASES

A phrase is a group of words that belong together and act as a grammatical unit.

PREPOSITIONAL PHRASES

A prepositional phrase begins with a preposition and ends with the noun or pronoun that answers the question What? or Whom? after the preposition. This noun or pronoun is called the object of the preposition.

> Jefferson's heritage *to the American people* was the Declaration *of Independence.* (to whom?...people; of what?...Independence)

> The stories *from the distant past* kept me spellbound. (from what?...past)

A prepositional phrase that modifies a noun is an adjective prepositional phrase.

> The noise *from the street* was deafening. (which noise?...from the street)

A prepositional phrase that modifies a verb, an adjective, or an adverb is an adverbial phrase.

> James went *for a walk.* (went where?...for a walk)

VERBAL PHRASES

A verbal is a word formed from a verb but not acting as the verb of a sentence. There are three kinds of verbals — the infinitive, the participle, and the gerund. Words added to these verbals make a unit of thought called a verbal phrase.

Infinitives

The infinitive begins with the word *to* and is followed by a verb.

> *To appear* on Broadway was her ambition.

To appear is an infinitive. *To appear on Broadway* is an infinitive phrase acting as the subject of the sentence.

> He hates *to be called* by his nickname.

To be called is an infinitive. *To be called by his nickname* is an infinitive phrase acting as the direct object of the verb (hates what?...to be called by his nickname).

Participles

Participles are verb forms that act like adjectives; that is, they describe nouns or pronouns. The present participle ends -*ing*; the past participle ends -*ed, -en, -d,* or -*t*.

> *Taking* no chances, Carol practiced daily for the tournament.

Taking is a present participle. *Taking no chances* is a participial phrase describing *Carol.*

> The picture, *painted* by Picasso in his youth, created a sensation.

Painted is a past participle. *Painted by Picasso in his youth* is a participial phrase describing *picture.*

161

Gerunds

A gerund always ends in *-ing*, and is used as a noun.

> *Following* through with his swing improved the golfer's score.

Following is a gerund. *Following through with his swing* is a gerund phrase acting as the subject of the verb *improved*.

> Burt enjoys *reading* mystery novels.

Reading is a gerund. *Reading mystery novels* is a gerund phrase acting as a direct object. (enjoys what?...reading mystery novels)

REMEMBER

Verbals are never used as the verb of a sentence, but they do have some characteristics of verbs. They can be modified by an adverb or adverbial phrase:

> Looking *pitifully about*, the mongrel searched for food. (looking how?...pitifully; looking where?...about)

They can be followed by direct objects:

> She loved to entertain *the neighbors*. (to entertain whom?...neighbors)

YOUR TURN

A. Identify the italicized phrases as prepositional, infinitive, participial, or gerund.

1. Sarah was assigned *to cover the play for the school newspaper.*
2. *Studying history* will help us *to avoid the mistakes of the past.*
3. The bracelet, *missing for days*, turned up *in the lost and found department.*
4. *Leaving just before sundown*, we hoped to avoid *driving in the heat.*
5. Poor people often dream *about ways to make huge sums of money.*
6. He claims *to have found a cure for baldness.*
7. *While studying ancient Egyptian manuscripts*, Mr. Banfi came across a formula which supposedly would grow hair *on the shiniest of bald domes.*
8. Police were called out *to maintain order* as the eager customers surged forward *to snatch at the remaining bottles on the counter.*
9. Since there is absolutely no scientific proof *of its effectiveness*, it is amazing that people are eager *to buy it.*
10. Bald-headed men, *willing to take a chance on any treatment* that promises *to restore their hair*, have made Andras Banfi a rich man.

B. Write a sentence with each of the following phrases:

1. Participial: having been chosen by a large majority   filled to capacity   stung by the cruel remarks
2. Gerund: seeing things clearly for the first time   passing a new tax bill   thinking about the day's events
3. Infinitive: to reach the summit   to be free of the responsibility
4. Prepositional: of the new technology   through the perils of outer space

Lesson 5
THE SENTENCE

What is a sentence? To understand what a sentence is, you must know two words — subject and predicate. A *subject* names a person or thing. A *predicate* makes a statement about the subject.

Complete subject	Complete predicate
A sudden shower	brought the game to a halt.

Within the complete subject, one word — *shower* — stands out as the key word. It is the simple subject. Within the complete predicate, one word — *brought* — stands out as the key word. It is the verb.

In the selection "The Guardian Angels," you read:

The original group was founded by Curtis Sliwa.

The complete subject of this sentence is *the original group*. The subject word is *group*. The complete predicate is *was founded by Curtis Sliwa*. The verb is *was founded*. (Lesson One explained that some verbs are made up of two parts, a main verb and a helping verb.)

COMPLETE SENTENCES

When you were in elementary school, you were taught the standard definition of a sentence: A sentence is *a group of words* containing *a subject and predicate* and expressing *a complete thought*. As you examine the three underlined phrases in the definition, you will realize why the concept of a sentence is one of the trickiest you will ever have to learn.

GROUP OF WORDS

Take the first item: a group of words. You may ask, "Must a sentence have a group of words? Isn't it possible to have a sentence of just one word?" Each of the following is a sentence:

Stand.   Eat.   Read.   Begin.

Each has a subject (*you* understood, but not written). Each has a verb (a statement made about the subject). Each expresses a complete thought. Nothing is left out.

On the other hand, the following statements, though they contain more than one word, are only parts of sentences, or sentence fragments, because they lack one or more of the essentials of a sentence.

THE ENGLISH YOU NEED TO KNOW

> Was about to be robbed (no subject: Who was about to be robbed?)
>
> When Johnson saw the teenager swagger through the subway train door at the 149th Street IRT station in the Bronx (incomplete thought: What happened when Johnson saw the teenager?)
>
> Curtis Sliwa, a 23-year-old manager of a McDonald's restaurant (no verb: What statement is made about Curtis Sliwa?)

You see, therefore, that a sentence can be very short, even one word, and a fragment can be quite long. Length alone does not make a sentence.

SUBJECT AND PREDICATE

You may also question the second part of the definition of a sentence: subject and predicate. The four one-word sentences above do not seem to have a subject. The words *stand*, *eat*, *read*, and *begin* are verbs. So you will have to say that when the subject is understood, as the word *you* before a command, it need not be written. The predicate alone is enough to make the sentence.

Also, the verb may be understood.

> Who has been helping to fight crime on the subways? The Guardian Angels.

Has been helping, mentioned in the question, is understood and mentally added to the subject in the response.

COMPLETE THOUGHT

Finally, you come to the third and most crucial part of the definition: a complete thought. Again, in certain cases, the subject and predicate may be omitted and mentally supplied by borrowing the exact words from a previous sentence.

> Have the Guardian Angels made the subways safer? Yes.

Yes can be considered a complete thought if you understand the sentence to read: Yes, the Guardian Angels have made the subways safer.

To conclude, a word or group of words cannot be a sentence if it does not express a complete thought. Compare:

> The frightened Johnson fished for his wallet.
>
> Just as the frightened Johnson fished for his wallet

The first group of words is a sentence because it has a subject (*Johnson*, the person you are talking about), a predicate (*fished for his wallet*, the statement made about the subject), and a complete thought. The second group of words is not a sentence. Though it has the same subject and predicate as the complete sentence, the addition of the words *just as* sets up a thought that remains incomplete. To complete the thought, the sentence must tell what happened just as the frightened Johnson fished for his wallet. Here is the complete sentence:

> Just as the frightened Johnson fished for his wallet, the car door opened and four fellows with red berets rushed in to seize the assailant.

Look at another example of an incomplete sentence:

> Showing the recruits how to spot a pickpocket

This group of words lacks the three elements of a sentence. It has no subject. Who is showing? It has no predicate. *Showing* is not a complete verb like *show, showed,* or *is showing.* In other words, even if there was a subject (like *he*), it would still be incorrect to call *he showing* a sentence. Lacking a subject and predicate, the group of words certainly does not express a complete thought.

To correct this sentence fragment, attach it to an already complete sentence and use the words *showing the recruits how to spot a pickpocket* to give additional — but not the key — information.

> He trains them in crime prevention techniques, showing the recruits how to spot pickpockets.

Another way to correct this sentence fragment is to give it a subject and a complete verb.

> He shows the recruits how to spot pickpockets.

YOUR TURN

A. Underline the complete subject and circle the complete predicate in each sentence:

1. The Magnificent 13, composed of a U.N. mixture of public-spirited youths, is rendering a unique service to subway riders.
2. Sliwa's 48 members all go to school or hold down jobs.
3. The police, distrustful of vigilantes, have not been too cooperative.
4. Having many loyal soldiers on our side makes us feel safe again.
5. Several interested people applied for the job.

B. Underline the simple subject and circle the simple predicate (verb) in each sentence:

1. New Yorker Arnold Johnson was about to be robbed.
2. It was 2 A.M.
3. Johnson saw the teenager.
4. He suspected trouble.
5. For more than six months the Magnificent 13 had been patrolling the dangerous routes.

C. Which of the following are complete sentences?

1. Pauline spent the summer in camp.
2. The furious storm rising from the dark sea.
3. Solving the riddle was no easy task.
4. With a roar of the engine and a whir of the helicopter blades.
5. At the stroke of midnight the alarm sounded.

D. Supply what is missing to make each of the following a complete sentence:

1. General agreement on the membership of the team.
2. Should use natural tones whenever possible.
3. Especially when giving a formal address before a dignified audience.
4. Since this introduction is not intended to cover everything.
5. Like placing the most important ideas in the most prominent positions.

PREDICATES

Sometimes a sentence needs only a subject and a verb to make sense:

> *Mr. Marin did* not *agree.* (The subject is *Mr. Marin.* The predicate verb is *did agree.*)

The meaning of this verb is complete without any additional words. Such a verb is called an intransitive verb. Other examples of intransitive verbs are:

> The truth sometimes *hurts.*

> He certainly *tried.*

> Please *sit* here.

> The dough *is rising.*

> The children *played* with the puppy.

COMPLEMENTS

Direct Object

Sometimes a verb needs a noun or pronoun to complete its meaning by answering the question What? or Whom? after it.

> He *used force* against the intruder.

The verb *used* is not complete without the word *force*, which tells what he used. Such a verb is called a transitive verb. The noun or pronoun that is the complement of the transitive verb is called the *direct object*.

> I called the *police* and got the *pistol.* (called whom?...police; got what?...pistol)

Indirect Object

A transitive verb may have another complement:

> He gave them a warning. (gave what?...a warning; gave to whom?...them)

In addition to the direct object, the verb has another complement, *them*, which answers the question To whom? Such a complement is called an *indirect object.*

Predicate Nouns

When the predicate verb is a form of the verb *to be*, a linking verb, or a verb of the senses, the verb may be followed by a noun or pronoun which re-states or re-names the subject:

> This is the last *straw.*

In this sentence a word in the predicate, *straw*, re-states the subject, *this.* Such a word is called **166** a *predicate nominative* or *predicate noun.*

Predicate Adjectives

Linking verbs may also be followed by an adjective which describes the subject:

The new law seems *unfair*.

Here, an adjective in the predicate, *unfair*, describes the subject. Such a word is called a *predicate adjective*.

REMEMBER:

—1.   Some sentences are complete with only the two essential parts, subject and verb:

The wind howled.

Democracy works.

Drugs kill.

Of course, in such sentences the subject or the verb or both can have modifiers:
The furious wind howled across the rooftops.

—2.   Other sentences require complements:

Daniel fixed the car. (fixed what?...the car)

Mr. Warren gave Henry another chance at the wheel. (gave what?...chance; gave to whom?...Henry)

—3.   The same verb can be transitive in one sentence and intransitive in another.
The use in a sentence determines whether it requires a direct object (transitive) or is complete by itself (intransitive).

Transitive: After a few days, Ben returned the book to the library. (returned what? book)

Intransitive: After a few days, Ben returned.

—4.   The same verb can be transitive in one sentence and a linking verb in another.
Linking verbs are followed by predicate adjectives or predicate nouns; that is, they link the subject with a noun or adjective in the predicate.

Transitive: Betty *felt* pangs of hunger. (felt what?...pangs)

Linking: Betty *felt* hungry. (Here, *hungry* is the predicate adjective because it describes *Betty*.)

All forms of the verb *to be* are linking verbs: is, was, will be, could be, might have been. So are these:

look	remain
seem	grow
sound	become
appear	turn
smell	prove
taste	stay

To test for a linking verb, substitute a verb *to be*:

> (Linking verb) The argument *remained* undecided. The argument *was* undecided.

> (Intransitive) Nothing *remained*. (*Was* cannot replace *remained*.)

YOUR TURN

A. Identify the italicized parts of the sentence as S (subject), V (verb), D.O. (direct object), I.O. (indirect object), P.N. (predicate noun), or P.A. (predicate adjective).

1. *Mr. Cannon*, a well-known attorney, *explained* the new *statute*.
2. Without it, every *citizen might think* that *he was John Wayne*.
3. Mr. Marin *is puzzled* by the attention his *case* has received.
4. *He told me* the *details* of the case.
5. Over 3000 *people have signed* a *petition*.
6. The *curtain* on that drama actually *rose* in Rome where Enrico Fermi *was born*.
7. It soon *became obvious* that he was a *prodigy*, an exceptionally brilliant child.
8. Fermi *received* the *Nobel Prize* in 1938.
9. Prof. Fermi *placed* a coded telephone *call* to his superiors at Harvard University.
10. *Dec. 2, 1992 will mark* the 50th *anniversary* of that landmark day.

B. Complete each blank with the part of the sentence called for:

1. Mr. Marin is a (P.N.) in New Jersey.
2. A man and a woman (V) his (D.O.).
3. The citizens gave (I.O.) the petition.
4. He was not (P.A.) of the problem.
5. The man (V) because he protected his (D.O.).

C. Tell whether the verb in each sentence is transitive (has a direct object), linking (has a predicate adjective or predicate noun), or intransitive (has no complements):

1. What should a man do in this case?
2. Somebody broke into his home.
3. The story appeared in the newspaper.
4. The thieves pleaded not guilty.
5. They ran to their car.
6. This case appears strange.
7. In this climate tensions increase.
8. The decision was unanimous.
9. He claimed self-defense.
10. The question remains unanswered.

D. Illustrate the following:

1. a fragment
2. a sentence that has only a subject and verb
3. a sentence with a direct object, indirect object or object of a preposition
4. a sentence with a predicate noun, predicate adjective or an appositive
5. a sentence with a linking verb

TYPES OF SENTENCES

PURPOSE

Sentences may have four purposes:

—**1.** A declarative sentence makes a statement.

Stuart plans to study computer science.

The car raced along the deserted road.

—**2.** An imperative sentence states a command, request, or direction.
The subject of an imperative sentence is *you;* it is usually understood.

(You) Take a few days to think it over.

(You) Do not swim beyond the raft.

(You) Follow the diet carefully.

—**3.** An interrogative sentence asks a question.
It is always followed by a question mark.

Where is Gate 7?

Are the children awake?

—**4.** An exclamatory sentence expresses surprise or a strong feeling.
It is always followed by an exclamation point.

How helpful the twins are!

What a glorious sight the tall ships made!

YOUR TURN

What kind of sentence is each of the following?
1. Hooray! We won the championship!
2. Let me show you how to walk onstage.
3. When will the mail come?
4. I can't wait for the mail to come.
5. Our country must find a sensible solution to the energy crisis.
6. Tina Bahadori had come to this country from Iran.
7. Is it fair to honor one of their nationals when they are holding our citizens hostage?
8. Don't sign the petition against the choice of Tina as valedictorian.
9. Do you think Tina was right in withdrawing her name?
10. American feelings toward Iran were inflamed because of the hostage incident.

STRUCTURE

Sentences have three basic structures:

—**1.** A *simple sentence* has one subject and one predicate.
Both the subject and the predicate may be compound, that is, composed of two or more similar
parts.

Flora excels in geometry. (One subject — Flora; one predicate — excels)

Joan and Maria are close friends. (Compound subject — Joan and Maria; one predicate — are)

Millions of stocks are bought and sold every day. (One subject — millions; compound predicate — bought and sold)

—2.　A *compound sentence* has two or more simple sentences joined by a comma and a coordinating conjunction (such as *and, but, or*) or by a semicolon.
Each simple sentence is called an independent clause; that is, it can be treated as a separate sentence beginning with a capital letter and ending with a period.

The plane has landed, but it will take time to get through customs.

Ken dribbled skillfully up the court; he swiveled and poured in the winning points.

—3.　A *complex sentence* has one independent clause and one or more dependent clauses.
A dependent clause has a subject and predicate but cannot stand by itself as a complete thought.

Carlos was delighted when he was chosen captain.

The independent clause is *Carlos was delighted;* the dependent clause, *when he was chosen captain.* The dependent clause has a subject, *he,* and a verb, *was chosen,* but it is not a complete thought. To complete the thought, the sentence must tell what happened when he was chosen captain.

YOUR TURN

A.　Tell whether each sentence is simple, compound, or complex.

1. The telephone rang just as the last guest left.
2. Dancers and actors generally require many years of training.
3. Bud pleaded for another chance, but it was no use.
4. Don't forget your pencil; a short pencil is better than a long memory.
5. As the votes were being counted, an air of suspense filled the room.
6. As Thomas Morley entered the cab for the ride to the airport, he was relaxed and serene.
7. During the next few hours, Mr. Morley aged rapidly.
8. I find things in my cab every day and I always return them.
9. Those little beauties would become the centerpiece of his collection.
10. It was cruelly ironic that those coins would have slipped through his fingers so easily.

B.　Compose an original sentence to illustrate each of the following:

1. a declarative sentence
2. an interrogative sentence
3. an imperative sentence
4. an exclamatory sentence
5. a compound sentence
6. a complex sentence

Lesson 6
WRITING EFFECTIVE SENTENCES

CLARITY

Writing implies that you have a message for someone. Your job is to make sure your message gets to your reader without distortion, alteration, or confusion. The poor writer will make errors or express only partial ideas, relying on the weak excuse, "You know what I mean." The successful writer will say exactly what he or she means and follow accepted standards of written English. Here are some guides to help you keep your sentences clear.

PRONOUN REFERENCE

Every pronoun must refer clearly to a specific noun or pronoun in the same or in a previous sentence. That noun or pronoun, called the antecedent, must agree with the pronoun in gender, number, and person.

Edward Adler had a mission in this world and *he* fulfilled *it*.

He (masculine gender, singular number, third person) refers to *Edward Adler*. *It* (neuter gender, singular number, third person) refers to *mission*.

The grateful nurse wrote to Edward's parents, telling *them* of *her* sorrow.

Them refers to *parents; her* refers to *nurse*.

Watch out for:

—1. Vague reference:

Delia told Georgette that *she* had *her* tennis racket.

The pronouns *she* and *her* could refer to either Delia or Georgette. The meaning is not clear.

Revised: Delia told Georgette, "I had your tennis racket."

Delia told Georgette, "You had my tennis racket."

There is no doubt as to the meaning in the last two sentences.

171

—2.   Shifting from singular to plural:

If *anyone* wants to join the chorus, *they* should come to the music office.

The pronoun *they* is plural; it cannot refer to a singular antecedent, *anyone*.

Revised: If *anyone* wants to join the chorus, *he* or *she* should come to the music office.

The pronoun and the antecedent are both singular.

If *you* want to join the chorus, *you* should come to the music office.

The pronoun and its antecedent are both in the second person *(you)*.

Anyone who wants to join the chorus should come to the music office.

The second pronoun has been eliminated entirely.

—3.   Reference of a pronoun to a group of words or a chain of ideas rather than to one word:

Doctors recommend regular exercise, *which* is why everyone should jog.

The relative pronoun *which* does not refer clearly to one specific word.

Revised: Because doctors recommend regular exercise, everyone should jog.

YOUR TURN

A.   Find the antecedent of the italicized pronouns. The first one has been done for you.

1.   Everyone was expected to complete *his* work on time. (antecedent: *everyone*)
2.   Won't someone volunteer *her* time for the registration drive?
3.   All the men and women at the meeting promised *they* would honor the picket line.
4.   Every member of the team must do *her* best.
5.   A person should choose a friend *he* or *she* can learn from.
6.   Mrs. Lyle was one of the parents *who* gave their children permission to go on the trip.
7.   Everybody, including the latecomers, enjoyed *himself*.
8.   Which one of the girls was elected to represent *her* class?
9.   This is the house *that* Jack built.
10.   "Martin," said *his* mother, "has been of enormous help to *my* sister."

B.   Choose the correct form of the pronoun.

1.   Neither of the women left (her, their) seat during the intermission.
2.   Each visitor gave (his, their) ticket to the guard.
3.   Everyone should have (his or her, their) blood pressure taken regularly.
4.   All of the 18-year-olds were ordered to register in (his, their) post offices.
5.   If anyone calls, tell (him or her, them) to send a resume.
6.   Some of the contestants ran (his or her, their) best races in this meet.
7.   Neither of the boys lost (his, their) temper.
8.   Each of the proposals must be judged on (its, their) own merits.
9.   Only Vera and Miriam managed to meet (her, their) quota of sales for the month.
10.   Laurie recognized one of the performers, but she didn't speak to (him, them).

C.   Revise each sentence so that each pronoun refers clearly to one word.

1.   Edward's father said *he* was an idealist. ("Edward was an idealist," said his father.)
2.   Edward Adler gave his life to save a nurse, *which* was a tragedy.
3.   Edward chased the attacker in *his* car.

4. Take the pictures from the shelves and dust *them*.
5. Maureen wants to be a doctor because *it* will give her a chance to help others.
6. In the newspapers *it* says that the strike is over.
7. Ted was improving, *which* pleased all his friends.
8. Leroy intercepted the pass, *which* was a lucky break for our team.
9. Dorothy has turned down three job offers. *This* is a mistake.
10. Sally told her mother that *she* has not received any phone calls that evening.

MODIFIERS

Every modifier must clearly refer to a word in the sentence.

Knowing that his techniques are effective, several school systems have invited the Reverend Jesse Jackson to address their students.

Knowing begins a participial phrase that modifies *school systems*. It is clear that school systems do the knowing.

The real reasons for his success are the potent ideas *that he communicates*.

The adjective clause *that he communicates* clearly refers to *ideas*. Watch out for:

—1. Misplaced modifiers:

The picture was drawn by Penny *hanging near the door*.

Was Penny hanging near the door, or was it the picture?

Revised: The picture *hanging near the door* was drawn by Penny.

—2. Dangling modifiers:

Being seasick, the waves seemed like towering mountains.

The participial phrase *being seasick* obviously refers to a person, not the waves, yet that person is not even mentioned in the sentence.

Revised: *Being seasick*, I felt the waves were like towering mountains.

Now the modifier describes the next word in the sentence, the subject *I*.

Since I was seasick, the waves seemed like towering mountains to me.

The modifying phrase has been changed to a dependent clause. Its subject, *I*, tells you who was seasick.

—3. Squinting modifiers:

Gary said *when he arrived* the game was over.

Did Gary get to see the game? Does the italicized clause modify *said* or *was*?

Revised: Gary said the game was over *when he arrived*.

Gary missed the game. The *when* clause clearly modifies *was*.

When he arrived, Gary said the game was over.

Gary probably saw the game. The *when* clause modifies *said*.

YOUR TURN

A. What word does the italicized expression modify? The first one has been done for you.

1. It is your attitude *that will determine your altitude.* (modifies *attitude)*
2. Jesse Jackson commands respect for the power of the messages *that he delivers.*
3. His motivational techniques are often far more effective than those *used by teachers.*
4. He tells it "the way it is," using language *that the listeners rarely hear from a school platform.*
5. *Smiling sweetly,* the hostess greeted the guests.
6. *When I was ten years old,* my family moved to Arizona.
7. *After reading the first few pages,* I couldn't put the book down.
8. The complimentary tickets *for the game* were mailed last week.
9. *Before the interview* Terry believed he had an excellent chance.
10. I regret that I have *only* one life to give to my country.

B. Revise the following sentences so that each modifier refers clearly to the correct word.

1. JoAnn met the man she was later to marry *in the library.* (In the library JoAnn met the man she was later to marry).
2. Do not give milk to a baby *that hasn't been pasteurized.*
3. Mario brought the papers to the editor *that had been misplaced.*
4. It is time to act *for men of good will.*
5. *While listening to the sad story,* my eyes filled with tears.
6. Sandy found her watch *walking along the beach.*
7. *Running to catch the train,* Van's books fell from his hands.
8. The family rented a substandard apartment *desperate for immediate lodging.*
9. *Saddened by the death of her dog,* a new pet was bought for Gail.
10. *Handling the wheel with skill,* the car was easily parked in the driveway.

C. Supply phrases or clauses to modify the italicized word.

1. *Walter* phoned his cousin.
2. Harvey *found* the locket.
3. The dentist examined the *x-ray.*
4. Orson rushed the *victim* to the hospital.
5. *All* had already been said.

CONSISTENCY

Use the same grammatical form throughout a sentence, avoiding any unnecessary shifts. Watch out for:

—1. Unnecessary shift in person

When one hears good news, *you* want to shout for joy.

The sentence begins in the third person (one) and switches to second person (you).

Revised: When you hear good news, you want to shout for joy.

—2. Shifts in tense (the time of the action)

The diploma not only *signifies* success in studies but also *indicated* good citizenship.

The first verb (signifies) is in the present tense; the second verb (indicated) shifts to the past tense.

> Revised: The diploma not only *signifies* success in studies but also *indicates* good citizenship.

> The diploma not only *signified* success in studies but also *indicated* good citizenship.

In both sentences the two verbs are in the same tense.

—3. Shift from active to passive voice or vice versa

> Aaron Morrison *keeps* referring to the law, but the law *has* often *been broken* by his own KKK throughout the last 150 years.

In the first clause, the active voice is used; that is, the subject (Aaron Morrison) does the action (keeps). In the second clause, the passive voice is used; that is, the action (has been broken) is done to the subject (law).

> Revised: Aaron Morrison keeps referring to the law, but his own KKK has often broken the law throughout the last 150 years.

The active voice is used in both clauses: Aaron Morrison keeps...KKK has broken.

YOUR TURN

Correct the unnecessary shift in person, tense, or voice.
1. If you follow directions, no one can miss the turnoff. (If you follow directions, *you* cannot miss the turnoff.)
2. If a student expects to pass, you should keep up with the homework.
3. When you buy clothing, a person should consider style, quality, and cost.
4. The witness took his seat at the table but refuses to answer any questions.
5. A good player gives his best at all times but consideration for teammates is not forgotten.
6. The administration knew about the energy crisis years ago but fails to offer solutions.
7. In accepting the nomination, the candidate spoke of America's strength, and the address was highly praised.
8. We were surprised when the door opened and in walks the principal.

PARALLEL CONSTRUCTION

Express parallel thoughts in the same grammatical form.

> That afternoon Rattan *informed* a sailor of an upcoming sea voyage, *predicted* a raise in pay for a bank teller, *told* a pregnant woman to expect a baby girl, and *cautioned* a motorcyclist about a possible accident.

The subject (Rattan) has four predicates, all in the past tense.

Watch out for:

—1.   Lack of parallelism in a series

The garage needed a cleaning, to be painted, and the roof had to be replaced.

The three things the garage needed are in three different grammatical forms. *Cleaning* is a gerund (a verbal noun ending in *-ing*); *to be painted* is an infinitive (*to* plus a verb); *the roof had to be replaced* is a clause (a group of words containing a subject and predicate).

Revised: The garage needed cleaning, painting, and roofing.

The same grammatical form (gerund) is used for all three parts.

—2.   Shift from noun to adjective or adjective to noun

Nancy is a *playmaker* and *excellent* in handling the ball.

Playmaker is a noun; *excellent* is an adjective

Revised: Nancy is a *playmaker* and an excellent *ball-handler.*

Playmaker and *ball-handler* are both nouns.

Nancy *is* a playmaker and *excels* in handling the ball.

Here the *and* joins two verbs, *is* and *excels.*

—3.   The use of *and which*

There is a sign on the door *and which* lists the doctor's office hours.

The *and* is not needed before *which.*

Revised: There is a sign on the door which lists the doctor's office hours.

A sign on the door lists the doctor's office hours.

The same grammatical form that is used before the word *and* should be used after it. In the original sentence, *and* is preceded by an independent clause (There is a sign on the door) and followed by a dependent clause (which lists the doctor's office hours).

—4.   Misplacement of correlative conjunctions, that is, conjunctions that come in pairs (not only...but also, both...and, neither...nor)

Babe Ruth *not only* was a home-run hitter *but also* a fine pitcher.

The same construction should follow both *not only* and *but also,* but in this sentence there is a verb after the first conjunction only.

Revised: Babe Ruth was not only a home-run hitter but also a fine pitcher.

YOUR TURN

A.   Correct the errors in parallel structure.

1.   They had both cookies for dessert and also there was ice-cream. (For dessert they had both cookies and ice-cream.)
2.   Kevin was not only athletic but he was a good student too.
3.   Sandra regarded all politicians as sly, not honest, and you cannot trust them.

4. There has been a change of heart either on the part of the champion or the challenger.
5. These are strange times for people who make movies, for people who pay to see them, and even the critics writing about them.
6. Doreen's volunteer service in a hospital was satisfying and gave her rewards.
7. Every comedian knows the importance of timing, and which can make the difference between success and failure.
8. At the grand opening sale, there were discounts on speakers, receivers, and you could also get tape decks cheaper.
9. My father is a man of great patience and who seldom raises his voice in anger.
10. Franz couldn't decide between taking chemistry or to switch to a shop subject.

B. Complete each blank with an idea expressed in the same grammatical form as the first item in each group or series.

1. The car needs a gas filter, _____, and _____.
2. Maureen likes not only tennis _____.
3. Don recalls seeing the stranger at the door, _____, and _____ .
4. Our city needs more parking space, _____, and _____ .
5. Barbara has a good sense of humor and _____.

C. Write an original sentence including at least 2 parallel thoughts on each subject.

1. Edward Adler's ideas on the duties of every citizen toward others. (Lesson 17)
2. Rattan Jeshi's wit and wisdom (Lesson 7)
3. Aaron Morrison's ideas on the American Constitution (Lesson 11)
4. Jesse Jackson's advice to adolescents (Lesson 12)
5. Your comments on one of the four people mentioned

COMPLETING THE THOUGHT

Do not omit important words that can change your meaning.

> My sister has *a* blue and white dress.

She has one dress with both colors in it.

> My sister has *a* blue and *a* white dress.

She has two dresses, one blue and one white. The repetition of the article *a* makes the difference.

Watch out for:

—1. Omissions of prepositions

> Jim was *appreciative* and *grateful for* the teacher's letter of recommendation. One can be grateful for but *not* appreciative for. *Appreciative* requires the preposition *of*.

> Revised: Jim was *appreciative of* and *grateful for* the teacher's letter of recommendation.

—2. Omission of *as, other,* and *else* in comparisons

> This winter was *as cold* if not colder than last winter.

Leave out for the moment the second part *(if not colder than)*. You now have an incomplete thought: This winter was as cold last winter.

> Revised: This winter was as cold *as,* if not colder than, last winter.

> This winter was as cold as last winter, if not colder.

Note the missing word in this sentence:

> Burton is taller than anyone on the team.

If Burton is on the team, the sentence is saying that Burton is taller than himself.

> Revised: Burton is taller than anyone *else* on the team.

> Burton is taller than any other person on the team.

The words *else* and *other* take Burton out of the group with which he is being compared.

—3. Illogical comparisons

> This year's taxes are higher than last year.

It doesn't make sense to compare taxes and a year. The sentence should be:

> This year's taxes are higher than last year's (taxes).

YOUR TURN

A. Add the necessary words that are missing from the following:

1. Jerry's grade in English is better than Susan but she excels in science. (Jerry's grade in English is better than Susan's but she excels in science.)
2. Little Jack liked the circus more than his father.
3. Cora never did like and never will be scolded.
4. Minna has no interest or desire to enter the dance contest.
5. Hortense is faster than anyone in her swimming class.
6. John can cook as well if not better than his wife.
7. California has a bigger population than any state in the union.
8. Tim's salary was only half as much as Jane.
9. The ink stains on my fingers were larger than my face.
10. Mrs. Purvis poured the milk into the cup and when full, gave it to her child.

B. Write your own sentences in which these words are followed by the correct prepositions.

1. curious
2. amazed
3. experiment (verb)
4. agree
5. aware

C. Write your own sentence with each of the following expressions:

1. as strong as...if not stronger
2. more useful than any other
3. more costly than
4. more troublesome than
5. most intelligent of

NEEDLESS REPETITION

Cut out words that do not add information.

> They returned Mr. Johnson's dentures (back) to him.

> I like to have as many loyal soldiers on my side as I can get (to help me).

The words in parenthesis are unnecessary since *returned* includes the idea of giving *back* and *to help me* merely repeats the idea of *on my side*

Watch out for:

—1.   Repetition of *that*

> The pitcher believed *that* if he tried a change of pace *that* he could fool the batter.

Eliminate the second *that*.

—2.   Wordy or roundabout expressions

> *The thing that worries me on the test* is the essay question.

The subject of the sentence is wordy.

> Revised: The essay question on the test worries me.

> What worries me on the test is the essay question.

—3.   Clauses that can be reduced to phrases and phrases that can be reduced to words

> *Since the Knights felt that victory was in their grasp,* they decided to freeze the ball for the final moments of play.

The clause can be reduced to a phrase.

> Revised: With victory in their grasp, the Knights decided to freeze the ball for the final moments of play.

Here is another sentence that can be reduced to a simpler form:

> Mrs. Rodriguez, *who is the president of the PTA*, promised to help with the Book Fair.

The clause (who is president of the PTA) can be replaced by an appositive.

> Revised: Mrs. Rodriguez, president of the PTA, promised to help with the Book Fair.

And one more example, this time reducing the clause to a single word.

> Pedro is a friend *whom I can always rely on.*

> Revised: Pedro is a *reliable* friend.

179

YOUR TURN

A. Rewrite the following sentences eliminating the unnecessary words.

1. In my opinion, I think the Olympic team should be supported by the government. I think the Olympic team should be supported by the government.
2. This new innovation in our school will solve the problem of lateness.
3. Several people in the class voted for a take-home final that could be done at home.
4. When the final bell rings at the end of the school day, come and meet me at the science lab.
5. Sam objects to eating in the cafeteria because the same menu is always repeated again and again.
6. Call the police immediately without delay.
7. Max thought that if he reviewed the chapter again that he would be ready for the test.
8. After she was interrupted, Selena continued on with her story.
9. As a rule Melissa always meets me at about three o'clock in the afternoon and we walk home together.
10. The beginning of the friendship started when Flo and Vera became neighbors.

B. Write a compact sentence — no repetitions and no omission of important elements — on each of the following:

1. a sports hero
2. a film star
3. a teacher you admire
4. a relative
5. a friend

C. Following the same directions as before, write a sentence expressing your opinion of:

1. school rules
2. New York City (or your home town)
3. a book you enjoyed
4. the drug problem
5. public transportation

STYLE

You must, of course, have something interesting to say in order to keep your reader's attention, but your subject and your ideas are not always enough. Your writing style is also important. If all your sentences are alike, their monotony will put your reader to sleep. You need to provide the variety that is the spice of style.

OPENINGS

Instead of starting every sentence with a noun used as the subject, begin with:

—1. Verb (inverted word order)

There *are* 25 different kinds of pies and cakes at the end of the line.

—2. Adverb

Nervously they had joked about breaking the bank at the roulette tables.

—3. Direct object

The jokes he had heard before.

—4. Modifiers

Cold and hungry, they wait on the line.

—5. Prepositional phrase

In their hands are the green vouchers which entitle them to a buffet.

—6. Infinitive phrase

To add a little zest to their lives, a steady stream of people wends its way to the gambling emporiums of Atlantic City.

—7. Participial phrase

Crossing at the corners, they head toward the buses for the journey back to civilization.

—8. Adverbial clause

As the heat still steams up from the pavement, the door of the casino opens wide.

—9. Absolute construction

The journey completed, they return home to recoup their losses and begin saving for the next trip.

Instead of a noun for the subject, use

—1. Gerund phrase

Hitting the jackpot is the gambler's dream.

—2. Noun clause

What they do not realize is that the cards are stacked against them.

SUBORDINATION

Not all thoughts or pieces of information are created equal. However, if you put them all in short, simple sentences, or if you string them together with *and* or *then*, the reader will assume that they are equally important.

Perry got the signal. He threw a low curve. It just nipped the outside corner.

The first sentence, being less important, should be subordinated to the second sentence. The last sentence can be reduced to an adjective clause.

> Revised: After Perry got the signal, he threw a low curve that just nipped the outside corner.

> After getting the signal, Perry threw a low curve that just nipped the outside corner.

You can use conjunctions to show the logical connection between pieces of information.

> The Hawks tried valiantly to catch up in the last quarter.

> The final buzzer found them trailing by three points.

The reader could probably guess how these are supposed to be connected, but readers shouldn't have to guess. Part of the writer's job is putting the information together in a way that makes sense.

> Revised: Though the Hawks tried valiantly to catch up in the last quarter, the final buzzer found them trailing by three points.

> The Hawks tried valiantly to catch up in the last quarter; however, the final buzzer found them trailing by three points.

The first revision uses a subordinating conjunction, *though*. Other subordinating conjunctions are *since, because, if, when, while, as*. The two sentences could also have been joined with the coordinating conjunction *but*. Other coordinating conjunctions are *and* and *or*. The second revision uses the conjunctive adverb *however*. Other conjunctive adverbs are *moreover, consequently, nevertheless, on the other hand*. Make sure you use the proper connective to show the relationship between two independent clauses or between a dependent and an independent clause.

Another example:

> Greg's mark on the exam was low *and* he had studied for many hours.

Since the two clauses aren't equal, *and* is the wrong connective. It should be replaced by a subordinating conjunction that explains the connection.

> Revised: Greg's mark on the exam was low *although* he had studied for many hours.

Although introduces a condition that leads to a conclusion opposite to the one expected.
Note: Be careful not to misuse *when* and *because*

> The best part is *when* the doctor turns out to be the murderer.

> The reason for the increase in gasoline prices is *because* OPEC wants higher profits.

These sentences use adverbial clauses beginning with *when* and *because*, where nouns are needed.

> Revised: The best part is the revelation that the doctor is the murderer.

> The reason for the increase in gasoline prices is OPEC's desire for higher profits.

The increase in gasoline prices is the result of OPEC's desire for higher profits.

Gasoline prices have increased because OPEC wants higher profits.

YOUR TURN

A.   Identify the grammatical structures used to begin the following sentences:

  1. When a professional ball game is over, the athletes retreat to their locker rooms to shower and change into their street clothes.
  2. Instead of concentrating on the story of the game, reporters were swept up with the excitement of which player strode by which female reporter in what state of undress.
  3. Now a blind woman can get a job as a sportswriter.
  4. Having voiced their opinions, the demonstrators returned to their homes.
  5. This rock Armstrong brought back from the moon.
  6. To prepare for the contest, Sarah practiced diligently every day.
  7. Speaking with the doctor brought the parents a feeling of relief.
  8. The renovation completed, we waited eagerly for the grand opening.
  9. What you see is what you get.
  10. Conveniently located and reasonably priced, the apartment was just what the couple had been looking for.

B.   Change the normal word order of each sentence by beginning with a word other than the subject.

  1. Fidel Castro is apparently throwing the hijackers in jail.
  2. The most unfortunate aspect of the loss for the Mets was the pitching failure.
  3. The child will be spoiled if you spare the rod.
  4. The escape route was somewhere below the cliffs.
  5. Faulkner, Hemingway and Steinbeck are among the American authors who have won the Nobel Prize for literature.
  6. The president's duties are to conduct the meetings and to appoint the committees.
  7. The dog, fearful and confused, would not follow the simplest commands.
  8. Applicants for the job must pass an examination to prove their ability.
  9. The night game abruptly ended when the power failure darkened the field.
  10. Cable TV is growing in popularity because the cost has come down.

C.   Combine the following sentences using the proper connectives:

  1. Felice has excellent coordination. She is the top gymnast in the school.
  2. Some of New York's subway routes are dangerous. The Red Berets wanted to stop muggers. They had been patrolling for several months.
  3. The speaker wore his leather jacket open. He wanted to show Johnson the gun. It was stuck in his belt. He slapped Johnson. The blow knocked out the man's false teeth.
  4. There was a highwayman. He had a sweetheart. Her name was Bess. He talked with her one night. The stable boy overheard the conversation. His name was Tim.
  5. In a few minutes they were all hypnotized by the same attraction. They were soon pulling the levers and dropping their chips on the dice tables. They were moving around in search of the pot of gold.

VARIETY

As you see, you can make your writing more effective by varying the beginnings of your sentences. Remember also to vary the length of your sentences so that your writing will be neither too choppy nor too complicated. While most of your sentences should be declarative, occasionally use the other types as well — imperative, interrogative, and exclamatory.

Declarative: The teenager told the man to give him the money quickly.

Imperative: "Let's have the money, and be quick about it," the teenager rasped.

Declarative: Mr. Konaplanik couldn't understand what the fuss was all about.

Interrogative: "What is all the fuss about?" asked Mr. Konaplanik.

Declarative: The father thought it was poor sportsmanship.

Exclamatory: "Some sportsmanship!" exclaimed their father.

In each case the change from the declarative form gives the sentence more snap and directness. It brings the reader closer to the action of the story and the feelings of the characters.

An effective composition also varies the basic structure of the sentences to include simple, compound, and complex sentences. Keep in mind the total effect of your writing. Too many simple sentences, especially short ones, can give a choppy, breathless effect. Too many compound sentences suggest a careless or lazy stringing together of unrelated ideas. Too many complex sentences can also become monotonous and sacrifice clarity and directness. The best combination is a proper balance of sentence types, in which the structure fits the meaning of the sentence and contributes to your overall purpose and intention.

Loose and Periodic Sentences

Another possible variation is the use of both loose and periodic sentences. In a loose sentence, the main idea is given before the actual end of the sentence. In a periodic sentence, the full meaning is withheld until the end.

Loose: He would have to bear the entire loss because his coins were not insured.

The loss, the important thing, is mentioned first; the reason, the lack of insurance, is not as important.

Periodic: Because his coins were not insured, he would have to bear the entire loss.

The main point, the loss, is withheld till the end of the sentence. Periodic sentences can be used to add emphasis and suspense to your writing.

Periodic: It was 2 a.m. when Johnson saw the teenager swagger through the subway train door at the 149th Street station, and he knew *that young man spelled trouble.*

Keeping this vital information for the end is more effective than a loose sentence would be:

He knew that young man spelled trouble when at 2 a.m. Johnson saw the teenager swagger through the subway train door at the 149th Street station.

Balanced Sentences

In a third type of sentence, a balanced sentence, the parts are of similar length and structure. The balanced sentence is an effective way of making contrasts.

The police haven't been too cooperative because they distrust vigilantes, but as one sergeant put it, "Let's face it, we're happy for whatever help we can get."

The conjunction *but* joins the two contrasting positions which are equally important. A balanced sentence comes at the conclusion of the Guardian Angels story.

> It's hard to predict how long the Guardian Angels will continue to render their unique service to subway riders but they are encouraged by the Arnold Johnsons of the city who say, "The boys make me feel safe again."

A famous line by the poet Alexander Pope illustrates the perfect balanced sentence:

> To err is human; to forgive, divine.

YOUR TURN

A.   Identify each sentence as declarative, interrogative, imperative or exclamatory.

1.   Could Mr. Morley remember the driver's name?
2.   Just then, up drove Mr. Konaplanik.
3.   Frantically, he sprinted to the door only to discover that the cab was gone.
4.   What a show!
5.   What should I do, be blackmailed for $76 worth of chocolate?
6.   Admit your guilt.
7.   I can't believe it.
8.   Look at the long life-line in this palm.
9.   Oh no, a lifetime dream wiped out in one careless act!
10.   "You have already been married," he laughed.

B.   Choose five of the above sentences and rewrite them as another type of sentence, for example, declarative to interrogative.

C.   Identify each sentence below as loose, periodic, or balanced.

1.   During the next few hours, Mr. Morley aged rapidly.
2.   It was cruelly ironic that they would have slipped through his fingers so easily.
3.   While cleaning out his cab, he discovered the brown box and returned it immediately to the St. Moritz Hotel.
4.   "What was all the fuss about?" asked Mr. Konaplanik as he pulled away from the curb.
5.   Once he got back to Cocoa, Florida, those little beauties would become the centerpiece of his collection.
6.   He received the lifelong gratitude of an astonished Mr. Morley, as well as a reward of $1000.
7.   I find things in my cab every day and always return them.
8.   He maketh me lie down in green pastures; He leadeth me beside the still waters.
9.   United we stand, divided we fall.
10.   The race is not to the swift, nor the battle to the strong.

D.   Choose five of the above sentences and rewrite them as another type of sentence, for example, loose to periodic.

E.   Write five sentences on one of the following topics using at least one of each type: declarative, imperative, interrogative, exclamatory.

An experience I'd rather forget

Space films are thrilling (or boring)

F.   Write five sentences on one of the following topics using at least one of each type: loose, periodic, balanced.

1.   What Parents Don't Know
2.   Just in Time

THE FINAL STEP

Now test yourself. As you skim through the following list of composition topics, try to recall or review what you have learned in the 30 lessons and the accompanying Handbook. Here are subjects to think about, talk about, write about. Decide on one that strikes your fancy, that sets your wheels moving. Write a first draft. Polish. Revise. Remember even the best writers work long and hard before they come up with a finished product. Here is a good place to start. The second composition will be easier and the next easier still. Good luck.

City of the future
Fairness in sports
Camping
Energy crisis
Safety in the schools
Back to nature
Old-fashioned ways
Sibling rivalry
Freshmen blues
Soap operas
Terrorism
Horror movies
If only I could
Women on the move
Crime victims
An unfinished project
The AIDS crisis
On the edge of tomorrow
Music in my life
What I learned from...
Just for the fun of it
A letter to my future grandchildren
The message of the Holocaust
Soviet strategy
Signs of spring
A conversation with Dad (Mom)
Modern miracles
Winning commercials
There ought to be a law
My favorite teacher (relative)
My first million
Democracy at work

INDEX OF VOCABULARY WORDS

The number indicates the lesson in which the new word appears.

P

palmistry (7)
patter (7)
peers (16)
penal code (16)
penalize (10)
penitentiary (12)
perilous (21)
persevere (19)
persistent (13)
perusing (29)
petitions (15)
philosophy (11)
plague (13)
plight (16)
polluted (19)
ponder (12)
potent (12)
pranks (18)
predicted (7)
presumably (5)
priority (22)
proctoring (29)
prodigy (22)
prohibited (25)
prolong (23)
protruding (18)
punitive (28)
pursued (24)
psychiatric (14)
psychologist (4)

R

racist (11)
radical (12)
ransacking (16)
rarely (4)
ration (6)
reactions (25)
readily (7)
recall (27)
recreation (5)
recruit (21)
regulations (1)
relentlessly (24)
render (17)
resent (4)
respectable (5)
retreat (25)
retroactive (30)
reverse (27)
risks (8)
rumpled (3)

S

saddled (15)
samaritan (17)
sanctuaries (25)
scold (1)
scores (14)
scrutinized (7)
segment (25)
serene (24)
shrewd (7)
signified (18)
slated (3)
smuggler (20)
spacious (3)
spectacle (10)
spectrum (27)
sprawling (17)
sprinted (24)
sputtered (30)
staccato (26)
staggered (1)
stakes (9)
statistician (19)
statute (16)
striving (22)
subordinates (30)
succumb (29)
sultry (3)
summoning (2)
surged (20)
survive (2)
sustaining (6)
swagger (21)
swerved (17)
sympathize (15)
syndicate (29)
systematically (6)

T

tardiness (4)
temporary (10)
temptation (29)
tension (9)
therapy (14)
thronged (25)
thrust (1)
thwart (21)
traditional (17)
transcribing (30)
transplant (13)
traumatic (14)
tuition (5)

U

ultimately (5)
unconscious (4)
unhampered (4)
unique (21)

V

valedictory (23)
vanished (2)
vehemently (16)
veracity (18)
verdict (30)
verify (28)
viciously (21)
vigilantes (21)
vile (19)
violate (11)
visible (27)
vivid (6)
voucher (3)
vowed (11)

W

welfare (8)
wracked (18)